PRAISE

Deep Talent is the book for now. The journey towards the skills-based organization is accelerating exponentially, driven by significant advances in AI. Garg, Ahluwalia, and Levit provide us with the roadmap for getting there.
Ravin Jesuthasan, bestselling author, recognized futurist and Global Leader for Transformation Services at Mercer

Enlightening, inspiring, and practical, *Deep Talent* is the guide for business and people leaders who want to understand and make sense of the massive shifts happening in the world of talent, learning, diversity, and technology, and their impact on the workforce in 2023 and forward. The authors provide a comprehensive framework to learn and operate in today's work world.
Enrique Rubio, HR thought leader and Founder of Hacking HR

Deep Talent is an essential read to help managers and leaders understand the accuracy and fairness of AI in the new world of work.
Laurie Ruettimann, HR thought leader and author of *Betting on You*

Organizations need both people and technology to grow and be profitable. *Deep Talent* is the must-read to bring these two forces together and create positive results. The real-world examples and case studies make it a resource that will never collect dust on your bookshelf.
Sharlyn Lauby, HR thought leader and Founder of HR Bartender

Deep Talent is a critical conversation worth reading if you value talent attraction, development, and retention in your organization. This book is for anyone who wishes to chart the most effective path forward in our new and evolving world of work.

Joey Price, President and CEO of Jumpstart:HR and host of *While We Were Working*

Deep Talent

How to Transform Your Organization and Empower Your Employees Through AI

Ashutosh Garg, Kamal Ahluwalia and
Alexandra Levit

KoganPage

First published in Great Britain and the United States in 2023 by Kogan Page Limited

2nd Floor, 45 Gee Street	8 W 38th Street, Suite 902	4737/23 Ansari Road
London	New York, NY 10018	Daryaganj
EC1V 3RS	USA	New Delhi 110002
United Kingdom		India
www.koganpage.com		

© Eightfold AI, 2023

ISBNs

Hardback	978 1 3986 0956 3
Paperback	978 1 3986 0954 9
Ebook	978 1 3986 0955 6

British Library Cataloguing-in-Publication Data

A CIP record for this book is available from the British Library.

Library of Congress Control Number

2022049967

Typeset by Hong Kong FIVE Workshop, Hong Kong
Print production managed by Jellyfish
Printed and bound by CPI Group (UK) Ltd, Croydon CR0 4YY

CONTENTS

FOREWORD

We live in a time of paradox. Technology is reinventing every job and industry, yet companies have a shortage of people. Organizations are automating work and focusing on employee experience, yet burnout and poor mental health are epidemic. Computers were supposed to reduce the number of routine jobs, yet retail, hospitality, and healthcare workers are almost impossible to hire.

What's going on?

Quite simply, we now live in a world of "talent limits." Every company, regardless of industry, has become a talent business, and the pace of change goes faster every day. Skills you learned two years ago are already becoming obsolete, and the job title or job description you love seems to be changing every quarter.

The answer? We need a smarter, more intelligent way to manage people.

A decade ago we talked about "integrated talent management" as the nirvana solution to leadership. We built competency models, assessments, nine-box grids, stack rankings, and all sorts of manual tools to help us hire, promote, and manage people through the company. Today almost all these artifacts have become obsolete. The replacement? A new set of technologies that Ashutosh and Kamal call "talent intelligence," smart and trusted systems that make work and organizations better.

I personally love this book, because it tells the story of Eightfold, and how two pioneering entrepreneurs took a lot of confusing tech and turned it into something we can use. AI, which has been the buzzword of the decade, was nothing more than a bunch of good algorithms five years ago. Today, through the forward thinking of this book's authors, we can use it and apply it for every talent problem we face.

I discovered Eightfold in its early days, and when Ashu and Kamal first explained it to me I was utterly confused. But over the last five years this company has pioneered, evolved, and now proved the result: deep learning and AI-powered talent solutions, coupled with massive amounts of data, can totally transform a company.

As you read this book you'll learn about deep learning, skills adjacency, and talent intelligence. You'll realize that they are easy to understand, important, and very powerful solutions today. And better yet, they can be applied to the public and private sectors and to all kinds of people in a variety of industries. So not only is this a book to teach you about how AI and big data can really make a difference, it also includes lots of examples and case studies you can use.

I've been working with Eightfold since almost the beginning, and this is a story about passion, ambition, and a never-ending intention to make a difference. Ashutosh and Kamal have invested in the technology, found the right applications, and are now revolutionizing the way we manage companies, starting from the people and moving out.

Let's say goodbye to the old-fashioned "talent management" practices that were designed to "manage the hierarchy." Now that organizations are entirely talent driven, tools like Eightfold's are indispensable for growth and competitiveness.

I hope you enjoy reading this story of the future that has suddenly become available today.

Josh Bersin
Global industry analyst
and adviser to Eightfold AI

ACKNOWLEDGMENTS

This book would not be possible without the year-long participation of an extremely dedicated team of people who are all so gifted at what they do. I'd like to take this opportunity to thank my co-authors, Ashutosh Garg and Kamal Ahluwalia, from whom I have learned so much, and Josh Bersin, who generously wrote our foreword and has been so supportive of this effort from the start. I am so grateful to Alex Cohen, Todd Raphael, and Ligia Zamora at Eightfold for your help with all things content and coordination. We quite literally could not have done this without you three. Much appreciation also goes to our editor, Matt James, Chris Cudmore, Arthur Thompson, Jaini Haria, and Shannon Branch. And finally, thanks to all the HR and workforce experts and practitioners who inspire me every day and permitted us to share their stories. We are so fortunate to have such a "deep" bench of talent from which to draw.

Introduction

After he wrote the world's very first resume, Leonardo da Vinci opened a world of possibility for those looking for meaningful employment.

At the end of da Vinci's ultra-practical resume, he humbly says, "I can paint as well." There's so much unrealized genius in that simple line, and it's exactly this type of potential we now have an unprecedented opportunity to realize in workers around the globe.

In our experience launching Eightfold—a software company currently valued at over $3 billion—and analyzing hundreds of millions of profiles to determine how people have moved in their careers, we believe the world is at a societal and technological inflection point. We're ready to empower employees to pursue the careers of their choice within our organizations.

How did we get here?

Amidst the Great Resignation and while the three of us were working on this book, Eightfold released a research study with Harris Interactive surveying 259 business leaders and 913 employees. The research sought to uncover the key HR priorities and objectives in today's business world, and how satisfied employees were with their current work offerings. We learned:

- Business leaders cite talent recruitment and development as top challenges due to talent shortages, long hiring times, and high turnover.

- Key challenges for employee engagement and retention include managing compensation expectations as well as providing employee expectations in line with post-pandemic norms.

- Employees consider company offerings centered on development to be most important (opportunities for promotions, effective performance reviews, transparent promotion and career development). The largest gaps in employee satisfaction with company offerings occur for these most important benefits.

- Employees express uncertainty over job fit as a top deterrent for submitting a job application, suggesting that opportunity exists to further optimize job listings.

- Technology is being employed to support DEI efforts but is notably not being leveraged for masked/blind resume review.

- A majority of leaders have already started to use AI for most HR functions, and most expect to increase investments in HR technologies in the near future.

Several workforce macrotrends were surfaced with these findings, and we'll discuss these in more detail in the first chapter. For now, though, we want to welcome you to *Deep Talent*. In the initial part of the book, we'll explore the different factors and perspectives at play in the larger arena of HR, talent, and workforce management.

Next, we'll describe the role of deep learning in the talent space and look under the hood of talent intelligence. We'll follow with a discussion of organizational learning and DEI applications and will then dive closely into how talent intelligence can be applied in global government and specific industry sectors. We'll conclude with how talent intelligence can be deployed on a much broader scale, including via our Workplace Intelligence Project.

In each chapter, we will spotlight company case studies, and you will have the opportunity to practice implementing ideas through working with a fictional company, FutureStrong.

We know from research and experience that nearly 50 percent of top talent leaves within two years, but also that most individuals would happily stay if given the right learning and growth opportunities.

Unfortunately, as companies grow and gain thousands of employees, CEOs tend to lose track of their workforce's abilities. They don't know what skills employees have already acquired at work, what skills employees are well equipped to master next, or how certain skills can be used to grow individual careers.

AI holds the promise of helping everyone in the world have a resume like da Vinci's, where the next big career accomplishment may be hidden in plain sight. In other words, the jobs are there, and the people are there. It's not an HR or a workflow problem, it's a matching problem.

The good news is, unearthing the right matches between the best people and the most critical jobs you need to fill is more than doable. The technology is here today, and the strategies needed to effectively wield it on behalf of our workforces are already being deployed across the globe.

AI is not something to fear but rather to embrace. Its existence means that fixing your labor shortages, hiring the best talent, and finding the right roles for your existing workers don't need to be a struggle for your organization any longer. And the journey starts with you.

When you see several authors listed on a book cover, you might be curious how they met and ended up working together. There are three of us, but the story starts with Ashu and Kamal.

Growing up in a small town in India, Ashu's parents raised him to believe that education is the most important thing and that he should do whatever it took to have the best schooling possible. His father traveled constantly for work and his mother stayed home to encourage her children's studies.

Ashu enjoyed computer science and specifically machine learning, and in 1998 determined that a PhD program in the United States was his best opportunity to solve big issues in the field and influence more lives than he would at home in India.

When he emigrated to attend the University of Illinois Urbana-Champaign, his friend Manish helped him settle in. It didn't take Ashu long to adapt to his new culture, and within a few years he was a living embodiment of the American dream: completing research, applying for patents, getting married and having children, and, of course, starting companies.

One venture is Eightfold. The company harnesses AI to solve the talent gap, a societal problem Ashu is deeply passionate about. Its name is inspired by the Buddhist Eightfold Path to Nirvana because Ashu believes that everyone has the right to choose how they want to earn their living—their career path.

Early in Eightfold's journey, Ashu met Kamal. Kamal had grown up in India too, but he'd spent nearly three decades in Silicon Valley with what he called a talent obsession. He was intrigued by Ashu and the former Google and Facebook execs who'd left those companies to create the first talent intelligence platform. Their goal? Marry the data available inside the enterprise with the data available outside in the larger market to match the skills workers have with the skills organizations require.

Ashu and Kamal built a company that now has more than 500 employees around the world and counts many among the Fortune 500 as customers. In 2021, when they decided to share their insights on talent intelligence with a wider audience, they looked for someone with experience writing business- and talent-focused books.

They found Alexandra, a *Wall Street Journal* columnist and author of *Humanity Works*, a book on the future of work. During their first meeting about *Deep Talent*, they felt a kinship: all three saw the promise of technology to facilitate more fulfilling human employment. They launched a collaboration that has so far spanned two years.

Talent is critical to success and skilling is paramount whether you are running an enterprise, a sports team, a hospital, or a nation. This book is for everyone who understands that employment is the backbone of our society, but that it's a hard problem to match the right people with the right roles. We are ready to empower you, the leader who cares deeply about talent, to leverage artificial intelligence to make the most work most meaningful to the most people.

By the conclusion, we promise you'll have learned exactly what to do to get there—not just for the benefit of your own organization but for the benefit of your own career and the careers of your friends, family members, the people who serve you and take care of your needs, and the members of future generations who are counting on us to transform what's possible when we think about jobs.

1

It's a matter of perspective

Kamal's daughter is in her mid-20s. She graduated from university, but like many in her age cohort, did not proceed with her career in the usual way. Taking advantage of the remote work trend, she has decided to live in three different cities consecutively. When she finds a place that feels like home, she might settle there permanently. Or, if she eventually outgrows that city, she might choose to move again.

She and her friends tell us that when it comes to jobs, they're searching for opportunities to explore. Although their parents have held between two and ten jobs over 40-year-long careers, Kamal's daughter's group wants to move much more frequently, with each move serving a purpose.

"I may only be in my 20s, but I've already seen a lot," she explained. "I know I only have one life to live, and I want the chance to try as many interesting things as I can. I don't want companies to look down on me for this, because ultimately I think I'll be a more well-rounded employee."

Speaking of Generation Z-ers who move around a lot, one of Kamal's daughter's current colleagues has had three jobs in three years. The second one, he'll readily admit, was not a good fit.

"This was a situation in which I just took what was next," he said. "It turned out to be the wrong opportunity; while I'm not opposed to taking risks, in the future I intend to accept offers having as much insight and information as possible so that my work is as fulfilling as I want it to be."

In this chapter, we'll explore the workforce macrotrends shaping the development and implementation of talent intelligence. We'll also hear from the individuals who can most benefit from changes in the way we hire, train, and deploy our talent, including organizational leadership, employees, and job seekers.

Workforce macrotrends in 2023

Prior to the pandemic, there was a good reason we called labor "human capital" and "human resources." The goal was to maximize employees' tangible contributions under whatever circumstances made the most sense for the bottom line.

We would hire contractors when we didn't want to pay benefits. We would offshore when we didn't want to deal with labor compliance. We automated functions as an excuse to lay off humans. Most employees didn't stay very long, but it didn't matter. When one person left, there were a dozen waiting to take their place.

But Covid-19, combined with natural demographic shifts (including baby boomer retirement and a small Generation Z) that are decreasing the overall size of the workforce, has upended work in a way we haven't seen in decades. Before we go any further in our discussion of talent intelligence, it's important to understand the overarching shifts impacting today's workforce.

Talent supply mismatches

Our global supply chain has been massively disrupted. Food, cars, chips, toilet paper, and even baby formula. We have the same issue with our talent. We don't know where to find it, whether we should hire someone internally or externally, and how long it will take to train them. When we don't have these answers, the uncertainty leads to cascading, short-sighted decisions, wasted resources on ineffective and outdated solutions, talent hoarding, and increased attrition.

It also leads to growing skills gaps. According to Deloitte's 2021 Human Capital Trends report, "the pandemic exacerbated growing digital, education, and skilling divides around the globe—putting further strain on talent supply considerations and trends" (Eaton et al, 2021). Deloitte found that the demand for skilled workers is growing rapidly, with seven in ten employers globally saying they are struggling to find workers with the right mix of technical skills and human capabilities, and that there are approximately half as many available workers per open position compared with a historical 20-year average.

Organizational consulting firm Korn Ferry noted this as well, suggesting that the world could face a talent deficit of 85.2 million workers by 2030 and a loss of $8.5 trillion in unrealized annual revenue (Binvel et al, 2021).

Meanwhile, in 2020, 80 percent of job losses were among the lowest quarter of wage earners, many of whom were working in the harder-hit sectors of hospitality and education.

It's estimated that around 100 million global low-wage workers will need to find a different occupation by 2030, and the market is ripe for transitioning to careers that are deemed more essential.

Consider the convenience store worker, a role that has traditionally had a low barrier to entry and minimal required training. During the pandemic and even today, convenience store workers have become rare and important assets.

During the pandemic, we also saw the genesis of the first employee exchanges and talent marketplaces, mechanisms by which employers could move workers from areas of talent oversupply to ones of talent undersupply—both between and within companies. This emphasis on skill development and retraining will come up time and time again over the course of the book!

Resignation and burnout

Talent supply has another significant problem, called "The Great Resignation." In mid-2021, Microsoft issued a shocking piece of research: over 40 percent of global employees were planning to leave their jobs within a year (Microsoft, 2021).

As a concept, the "Great Resignation" was initially proposed by Anthony Klotz, a management professor at Texas A&M University.

In 2021, Klotz predicted that once the pandemic ended and life returned to normal, the workforce would see a huge exodus of employees re-evaluating their careers.

This re-evaluation prompted workers to realize that they weren't actually enjoying the work they were doing, and considering that 80 percent of people apply to the wrong job, this wasn't surprising and it was only a matter of time before they decided to do something about it. And because compensation was not the prime motivator for a lot of these folks, financial perks from their current companies didn't necessarily help.

A 2021 *Harvard Business Review* study led by Visier's Ian Cook confirmed that by mid-2021, companies had a record number of open positions. Resignation rates were highest among mid-career employees and in the technology and healthcare industries (Cook, 2021).

Although having the wrong job in the first place is absolutely driving moves, burnout can't be ignored as a critical factor. Although some escalation was expected during the throes of the pandemic, it's troubling that burnout has become a seemingly permanent issue. As recently as mid-2022, only 33 percent of workers said they were thriving in their overall well-being.

Working parents have undoubtedly been hit the hardest. When family health organization Maven and Great Place to Work surveyed 500,000 workers, they found that one in four working parents was experiencing active burnout at work.

"Even as schools and childcare centers reopened, parents continue to navigate additional health and safety precautions for their kids," Maven's senior vice president of people Karsten Vagner told CNBC in late 2021 (Liu, 2021).

Maven's report illustrated that working mothers, and particularly mothers in under-represented groups, were more likely to experience burnout due to lack of support and recognition in their career, ranging from unequal pay to stalled promotions. Approximately 1.4 million mothers of school-age children left their jobs or were forced to change careers during the pandemic.

Considering that much of this burnout is a direct result of juggling inflexible work with parenting schedules, Maven and Great Place to Work found that nearly five million cases of burnout are "preventable." And only some organizations answered their employees' calls for help.

Even in Asia, a region known for its extreme work ethic, many employees have had enough. Deloitte's 2021 Human Capital Trends report noted that in Asia, "some workers are actively revolting against the pressure to work themselves to death by adopting an ethos of 'lying flat'—a movement that espouses lying down, both literally and metaphorically, instead of joining the rat race of professional advancement" (Eaton et al, 2021).

Broader talent sourcing

In response to talent supply issues, many organizations are getting more creative and open-minded about their sourcing strategies. Insisting that every employee have a four-year college degree and an exhaustive list of competencies no longer works. Your positions will simply remain unfilled.

According to McKinsey's late 2021 piece "The Great Attrition: What to do about the labor shortage," authors De Smet, Dowling, Hancock, and Mugavar-Baldocchi suggested that organizations re-examine job requirements to broaden the potential candidate pools. "Given that unemployment is still relatively higher for younger workers, those without a college degree, and those returning from prison, companies can expand their candidate pool by finding ways to tap into these segments," they wrote (De Smet et al, 2021).

We're also seeing a significant uptick in boomerang hires, or individuals who worked for an organization before, left on good terms, and kept in touch through personal contacts or alumni network events.

Advances in talent intelligence can lend a helping hand, processing three billion pages of data a day—much faster than a recruiter can examine individual LinkedIn profiles! We will cover this in further detail in the next chapter.

As we'll discuss throughout the book, AI algorithms prioritize "soft" factors in hiring, curating candidate data from publicly available data forums such as Google and AngelList to learn about each potential candidate's learning styles, motivators, and workplace values. The more organizations adopt AI-driven sourcing systems, the greater our overall potential to provide meaningful work opportunities to underserved groups.

Job redesign

When you hear the words "job redesign," you might think of the hybrid work approach that many organizations adopted with the Covid-19 pandemic. Gallup's 2021 *State of the Workforce* research found that more than half of US professionals prefer to split their time between working at home and onsite (Pendell, 2022).

Even when it was once again considered safe to congregate in a building, hybrid work didn't go away. Companies had listened to their employees, and they also recognized the benefits for themselves.

Gartner's report, *Redesigning Work for a Hybrid Future*, discussed that "executive leaders now have a unique opportunity to break from a location-centric model of work designed around industrial-era constraints, and to redesign work around a human-centric model" (Gartner, 2021).

A human-centric model is not just a nice-to-have. "Human-centric work design, characterized by flexibility and empathy, makes employees feel more empowered, and increases their productivity and engagement," wrote the Gartner authors. "It also enables organizations to be more responsive to customer demand, more resilient to disruptions and more productive. It can also reduce a range of costs—from real estate and travel to employee attrition."

Naturally, one of the next questions for leaders is, "how do we create an in-person space that supports an effective hybrid work culture?" In their 2021 article for *Harvard Business Review*,

Steelcase CEO Jim Keane and Gensler managing director Todd Heiser advised that optimal collaboration occurs in open spaces with movable boundaries and enclosed, pod-like spaces so you can balance the need for group work and individual work that requires privacy and focus (Heiser and Keane, 2021).

Hybrid work has also pushed an agenda that workforce futurists have mulled for more than a decade: the need to redesign jobs so they align with digital transformation.

Increasingly, organizations are creating job categories for the oversight and management of machine partners and the integration of human and machine labor. This redistribution of effort keeps "humans in the loop" to provide creativity and strategy as digital components focus on the task-oriented, routine, and repeatable work at which machines are best. We're also seeing the rise of "superjobs," which are a mashup of components from traditionally separate jobs and often cross departmental fault lines.

For example, in the legal realm, a "case synthesizer" might combine the jobs of database administrator (IT) and paralegal (core business) to examine legal precedents mined by an algorithm and handpick the most critical ones for the case at hand.

Job redesign is also governed by current skills and labor short-ages. As this book is mostly about skills, this won't be the only time we suggest that simplifying and deconstructing jobs into skills is a sound strategy to take stock of the work being performed today, understand redundancies, and promote the skills that are actually essential.

Leah Johnson, Gartner vice president of advisory services, addressed the sourcing issue we mentioned earlier. She commented that organizations are realizing the hurdle of trying to fill roles with an increasing number of talent dependencies. "This competency creep typically includes so many technical and soft skills that it becomes a Herculean task for recruiters to source talent among limited pools," she wrote (Gartner, 2019).

Johnson cited the example of the data scientist role. "Organizations increasingly tend to look for the rare combination of technical, data visualization, and high-level communication skills in one person when filling a data scientist role," she said.

In the best job redesign efforts, the organization identifies the competencies needed for data scientists and then breaks the role down into much smaller tasks and skills. At this point, they might source different candidates for specific aspects of the role, and such candidates could include full-time employees, employees who are working part-time in another area, or contractors.

This process is a bit more complex than lumping the stars, the sky, and the sea into a single job description, but it gels nicely with the human-centered and flexible hybrid work model that appears to be here to stay.

Focus on employee growth and well-being

An old adage goes: "Choose a job you love, and you will never have to work a day in your life."

If you are not enjoying your work or feeling like you are accomplishing something, every hour is a drag. But what if an employer treated you like family? What if there was solid alignment between company goals and personal aspirations? What if a company created an environment where everyone was in this thing together?

In keeping with the longstanding view of employees as commodities, most organizations have been unaccustomed to concerning themselves with aspects of employee lives outside what they do between office walls.

The pandemic necessitated a more holistic view of the employer and employee relationship. Generation Y and Z-ers had been telling us for years that they wanted their companies to treat them like family, but suddenly, employer actions to promote employee well-being were under a microscope.

According to Jeanne Meister, founder of Executive Networks' company Future Workplace, there are five primary levers of employee well-being that organizations are now required to address: *financial* well-being (compensation and education), *mental health* well-being (employee assistance programs, access to therapy), *social* well-being (company culture and work/life balance), *physical* well-being (workplace safety and exercise programs), and *career* well-being (access to training and coaching) (Meister, 2021).

While all of these levers are important, a 2021 Future Workplace survey found that mental health has taken center stage. Approximately 68 percent of senior HR leaders rated employee mental health as a top priority.

And per the Kaiser Family Foundation, nearly 40 percent of employers updated their health plans after the start of the Covid-19 pandemic to expand access to mental health services and increase the ways in which workers can get mental health services, including telehealth access (Kaiser Family Foundation, 2021). Many organizations have also ramped up manager training designed to support individual employee needs while maintaining their own well-being.

Inclusion and advocacy struggles

Back in 2017, global management consulting firm PwC convened a group of CEOs to sign a pledge to elevate and support a more diverse and inclusive workplace by cultivating environments that support an open dialogue around these issues.

In the years since, the pledge has expanded to include the concept of workplace belonging, which is the feeling of security and support when there is a sense of acceptance and identity for a member of a certain group.

By mid-2021, almost 2,000 CEOs at companies from Verizon to McDonald's had made this public commitment, in part due to the number of young workers and minorities who were disproportionately impacted by the pandemic and subsequent layoffs.

PwC research showed that the pledge is making a difference. Seventy-five percent of leaders said they were investing in DEI (diversity, equity, and inclusion) initiatives to meet the expectations of customers, stakeholders, and investors (PwC, 2021).

But one-third of respondents admitted that diversity was still a barrier to progression at their organizations and 80 percent said leadership engagement on DEI remains at a basic level. Just 25 percent of organizations have specific DEI goals for leaders, only 17 percent have a C-suite level diversity role in place, and 31 percent have no leader for DEI programs at all.

The use of data analytics to improve DEI outcomes is also not as pervasive as it could be given the sophistication of available technology. In the PwC research, 80 percent of respondents said their organizations had not tackled unconscious bias by collecting compensation, hiring, performance, and promotion data. And only 30 percent said they analyzed data across different diversity dimensions.

Struggling with DEI is not a good look for companies that want to attract and keep top talent. According to PwC, 86 percent of women and 74 percent of men seek employers with clear diversity and inclusion strategies.

Workers have noticed that progress isn't where it needs to be. Following the death of George Floyd in 2020, a Benevity poll found that 61 percent of employees believe their companies have not fulfilled their stated commitments to address racial justice and equity issues (Benevity, 2021).

Employees want their companies to take a stand on political issues too. In 2021, for example, cryptocurrency company Coinbase adopted an "apolitical culture." Coinbase said it would not debate causes or political issues unrelated to work, represent personal beliefs externally, or take on activism outside of its core mission at work. It promptly lost 5 percent of its employees.

It wasn't surprising. Eighty-six percent of global respondents in the 2021 *Edelman Trust Barometer* research reported that they expect CEOs to publicly speak out about societal challenges (Edelman, 2021).

Employee experience and flexibility

Related to job redesign and the rise of hybrid work is employee experience. Over the last few decades, employee experience has risen to the forefront as an essential part of engagement over the employee lifecycle—from talent acquisition to onboarding to learning and development, performance management, and offboarding.

Recent McKinsey research indicated that a poor employee experience is responsible for much of today's attrition, and prior to the pandemic, many organizations launched "high tech/high touch" connection points to navigate the employee experience and ensure that new hires feel bonded and assimilated (Chodyniecka et al, 2022). For instance, in the onboarding phase, a company might provide orientation materials digitally along with a manager script to facilitate a one-on-one check-in with the new hire.

Post-pandemic and beyond, companies are making progress customizing their employee experiences to different groups depending on their unique journeys and requirements. We know, for instance, of a few organizations that have full lifecycle employee experience initiatives for their contract and seasonal workforces.

The 2023 employee experience focuses on two overarching themes: purpose and flexibility. Employers have recognized that when people view their work as meaningful and their contributions as valuable, they will be more engaged and productive, and will also stay longer. One component of purpose is knowing where one can use current skills, and how to acquire new skills for the next chapter.

Purpose also ties into inclusion and well-being. Workers who feel cared for and like they belong through the employee experience are also more likely to feel secure and comfortable with their place in the organization.

The concept of flexibility within the employee experience is also maturing. Even with the rise of hybrid and remote work during the pandemic years, much flexibility talk was reserved for knowledge workers.

Now, though, flexibility is a cornerstone of every employee's experience. Just because a worker is deemed "essential" and/or needs to be onsite doesn't mean flexibility is a non-starter.

There are several ways to integrate more flexibility into the frontline worker experience. You can offer employees the ability to schedule and switch their hours, as well as the location at which they work and the colleagues with whom they work. You may also allow workers to choose whether they work four ten-hour days rather than five eight-hour days.

This hyperfocus on individual employee needs is novel—and complicated. "Management should not overlook training. Much of this flexible work model is still new to everyone," wrote Carl Olivier in a 2021 article for *Fast Company*. "Employees might need to learn new skills, new processes, and new technologies. By investing in quality training programs, companies can avoid problems down the road" (Olivier, 2021).

Allowing current and potential employees to contribute to an organization in a way that makes sense for all parties is another important dimension of flexibility. As an example, the US Department of Defense has developed Gig Eagle, a platform to locate skills that are currently undiscoverable, such as compliance and adaptability in the face of adversity. It's similar to Uber and Airbnb in that one million reservists and members of the National Guard can put their knowledge and skills to use on DoD projects.

Sarah Pearson leads commercial efforts for AI and machine learning at the DoD's Defense Innovation Unit. As she told us at our recent Cultivate conference, in its simplest form, the DoD is creating its own gig economy. "We are uniting part-time military members with short-term needs inside the DoD. For instance, if we have a marine reservist and they happen to be a partner or a principal at a tier 1 VC, I would appreciate their help on my team. Gig Eagle helps us connect the skills that military members have gained or are gaining in the private sector for their benefit and the benefit of the DoD."

We will hear more about Gig Eagle in Chapter 6, but once again, it comes down to skills.

SPOTLIGHT ON PRUDENTIAL
Global insurance company confronted talent supply mismatches by using AI to uncover skills within its ranks.

Prudential Financial is a US Fortune 500 company whose subsidiaries provide insurance, retirement planning, investment management, and other products and services to both retail and institutional customers around the world.

While grappling with the current talent crunch, Prudential decided to leverage internal mobility to upskill and reskill its existing employee population. HR leaders started by participating in a strategic planning process that unearthed the company's required capabilities. Armed with these capabilities and the associated skills, Prudential leveraged a talent intelligence platform to identify how and where people with a certain skill set could be redeployed.

"The goal was to uncover what people might want to do that they've already done or haven't had exposure to before. We never had this information before because organizations tend to have tunnel vision," Vicki Walia, chief talent and capability officer at Prudential, told us at the Cultivate conference.

First, Prudential built skill profiles for its employees so the data existed to better understand how to grow and develop them. Next, the HR team made an impactful policy change, mandating use of the new internal talent marketplace. Every opportunity has to be posted for everyone to see, and hiring managers must keep the role open for two weeks to democratize the application process. When an employee throws their hat in the ring for an internal position, their current manager is now made aware that the employee can do certain things the manager might not have known about.

"Our working hypothesis was: if we create accessibility to and transparency with open positions, we will see more diverse pipelines," said Walia. "And sure enough, the greatest users of the internal mobility platform are black women from the ages of 39–49. They're also the most satisfied users."

Prior to the use of talent intelligence, Prudential's internal mobility rates were approximately 38 percent. Today, they hover around 55 percent, and around 48 percent of all global employees have taken advantage of a new opportunity.

Employee listening

Starting with the annual employee survey, employee listening and organizational feedback vehicles have been in place for some time. However, as organizations become more dispersed and collaboration technology increases in sophistication, companies are tapping employees for input at more frequent cadences.

Employee listening strategies like surveys, internal social media, and focus groups are now routine for keeping tabs on sentiment. Adding surveys at key points in the employee experience, such as the first interview, the first project completion, and the first performance review, allows employees to give feedback at scale and organizations to course correct based on that feedback. Of course, such surveys require sensitivity, because most employees are somewhat reluctant to share negative feedback with leaders and prefer it be collected anonymously.

Employee resource groups (ERGs) can be a terrific source of intelligence if members are willing to provide it. In particular, many companies are soliciting diverse employee opinions on organizational rituals and norms to ensure they feel welcome and included. For instance, a company may learn through an ERG focus group that non-binary employees would prefer a change in restroom configuration.

The shift to a hybrid workplace where it's more challenging to keep track of people has elevated the importance of employee listening. Rather than issuing a mandate for all employees in a given office or department to engage in the same way, organizations need to take individual employee pulses regarding what's working in terms of work structure and environment—and what isn't. They can also expect these opinions to change frequently.

Here's some good news. In the last few years, organizations have become more adept at hearing a concrete suggestion based on a firsthand perspective, rewarding the employee for sharing it, and doing everything in their power to implement it.

The other side of the employee listening coin is the sometimes-maligned employee monitoring. Especially with the rise of remote work, many organizations have installed digital tools to track employee productivity, work product, and social interaction.

According to Deloitte's 2021 *Human Capital Trends* report, one out of four companies purchased new technology during the pandemic to passively track and monitor their workers, and 95 percent of IT leaders increased the frequency of worker listening. The Deloitte authors warned that these activities "may cross the line into worker surveillance, raising potential risks around data privacy" (Eaton et al, 2021). And one has to worry that these developments will breed distrust between workers and their employers—resulting in decreased engagement and retention.

Compliance and government regulation

During and in the aftermath of the pandemic, HR compliance has risen to a never-before-seen level of complexity. While more than 2,000 legislative updates related to Covid-19 streamed in across the globe, employers struggled to keep up with the policies they needed to update or create.

Some organizations needed compliance guidance around laying off or furloughing employees, reducing hours, taxing remote workers by the appropriate jurisdictions, or closing businesses or locations. Others looked to the government to provide direction on maintaining a safe work environment and adhering to laws designed to prevent discriminatory practices, such as the Americans with Disabilities Act, during vulnerable times.

Then, once the world began to recover, compliance issues arose associated with re-opening, distributed work, travel, vaccination, testing, PPE mandates, and pandemic-prompted benefits.

According to ADP's Ellen Feeney in an article for Corporate Compliance Insights, her team's data showed that employer calls for advice on compliance questions jumped more than 1500 percent in 2020 and 2021 (Feeney, 2021).

Organizations operating cross-nationally have arguably experienced the greatest headaches. "With different areas of the world experiencing various phases of the global health event, businesses needed to follow all applicable guidance and regulations relevant to their locations, presenting a unique challenge to navigate," Feeney wrote. "To stay compliant, many companies relied on local employees who were closest to timely updates and leveraging technology to automate the process."

Much of the world has been surprisingly supportive of increased government regulation. In Deloitte's *2021 Human Capital Trends* research, government regulation was cited as the most influential external factor behind an organization's ability to thrive (Eaton et al, 2021).

Why? One might say governments can take some of the pressure off employers. "Government effectiveness in driving social change, such as policies around worker representation or protection, or actions to address concerns such as climate change or social injustice, could shift workers' expectations of their employers to attend to such issues," wrote the Deloitte authors.

"Public policy and regulation protecting jobs and wages, enhancing social safety nets and benefits, improving access to education, or investing in reskilling could decrease workers' reliance on their employers for these things."

One area of specific concern is the gig economy, which is a labor market characterized by the prevalence of short-term contracts or freelance work as opposed to permanent jobs.

According to research published by the US publication *Small Business Trends*, the gig economy grew by 33 percent in 2020, expanding 8.25 times faster than the US economy as a whole (Pickard-Whitehead, 2021).

The same year, two million Americans tried gig work for the first time, and 34 percent of US workers are now involved in the gig economy. Four in five businesses are planning on hiring more gig workers post-pandemic, with 50 percent saying they have already done so.

As organizations tried to manage their gig workforces with internal and external digital talent marketplaces and enhancements to the gig employee experience, many ran into regulatory and compliance issues and steep penalties for misclassifying employees.

In 2020, when the US state of California attempted to require companies to classify gig workers as employees, gig-driven companies responded with Proposition 22, which aimed to keep gig workers classified as independent contractors.

Although that specific law was eventually ruled unconstitutional, the battle isn't over in the US or in the EU.

As we write this, gig workers in the EU often find themselves in court, needing to prove that they deserve basic employee rights. The European Commission is in the process of finalizing legislation that will shift the burden of proof on employment status to companies rather than gig workers.

As part of the new law, gig-driven companies like Uber and Deliveroo will need to pay workers the minimum wage and also provide sick days, paid holidays, and other benefits typically reserved for full-time employees. It will be interesting to see how this develops.

Of course, this wouldn't be a book about artificial intelligence or with a section on compliance without mentioning the need for "responsible AI." For a bit of background, in the United States and some other countries, adverse impact refers to employment practices that appear neutral but have a discriminatory effect on a protected group. It can occur in hirings, onboarding, learning and development, and firings or layoffs.

In response, the US government adopted a "four-fifths" or "80 percent" rule. To assess whether a selection procedure violates the four-fifths rule, the selection rate for the group with the highest selection rate is compared to the selection rates for the other groups in the pool. If any of the comparison groups do not have a selection rate equal to or greater than 80 percent of the selection rate of the highest group, then you have evidence of adverse impact for this selection procedure.

Also in the US, the Department of Labor's Office of Federal Contract Compliance Programs (OFCCP) enforces the non-discrimination and affirmative action obligations of federal contractors and subcontractors to the federal government. It is unlawful for those doing business with the federal government to discriminate against workers based on race, color, religion, sex, sexual orientation, gender identity, national origin, disability, or status as a protected veteran in any aspect of employment.

A related organization, the US Equal Employment Opportunity Commission (EEOC), is the agency responsible for enforcing federal laws regarding discrimination or harassment against a job applicant or an employee. It was formed by Congress to enforce Title VII of the Civil Rights Act of 1964. Both organizations are continuously updating policies to protect the most vulnerable applicants and employees in our organizations, and if implemented properly, AI can go a long way to help.

To prevent adverse impact and ensure compliance with the "four-fifths" rule as well as OFCCP and EEOC guidelines, AI-based technologies must have proper human oversight. They must be tested pre-deployment and regularly audited to check against biases before implementing any changes to the algorithm. Through validation methods such as candidate masking and statistical parity, as well as a skills-only approach to candidate assessments, AI-based technologies can provide reliable measures for mitigating biases and help organizations address OFCCP and EEOC obligations.

Perspectives across the workforce

Macrotrends are based on general sentiment, but sometimes research alone makes it difficult to see talent issues from all relevant angles. By telling the stories of individuals experiencing today's workforce through a variety of lenses, we can add color and meaning to the challenges we must, at the end of the day, address as a team. Let's start with Liva.

The CEO

Liva is the 52-year-old CEO of a mid-sized manufacturing supply company headquartered in the United States with offices in a dozen other countries and nearly 25,000 employees. She "grew up" in the organization, starting as a regional salesperson when she was in her late 20s.

Liva's company touches several transforming industries. As healthcare moves online, automotive relies more on computerized components, finance becomes fintech, and retail and hospitality shift their distribution and service vehicles, Liva finds that her workforce lacks the skills to evolve with her customers.

Suddenly, Liva's clients want equipment and service she has never had to provide before. Digital transformation and automation hold so much promise, but Liva doesn't understand how to implement or oversee new technology appropriately.

Despite ramping up her talent acquisition efforts with her HR department of 15 and targeting specific skills gaps, Liva has been mostly unable to find hires with the skills to keep the company moving in the right direction. No matter how much compensation Liva prepares to offer, the talent simply isn't there.

And although Liva recently acquired a small automotive parts manufacturer, she doesn't have a handle on the skills and experiences the new company's employees have and what they are capable of doing if given the opportunity. This is especially difficult to assess given that all of Liva's non-factory jobs now have a hybrid structure.

Liva recognizes the need to upskill and reskill the people both in her original and new companies—provided they are willing to stay. These upskilling initiatives will teach employees to do the jobs they have better or more efficiently. Reskilling will teach them to do new jobs.

Liva is acutely aware of the employee churn over the last two years, especially among diverse employees. Her board members are rightfully questioning this, insisting that they will hold Liva accountable for social responsibility initiatives that result in tangible progress.

But she feels helpless. Today's employees have more autonomy and control than ever. Liva became CEO at a time when she didn't have to focus on individuals because the company held all the power.

Liva is also worried about the SEC's recent change to Regulation S-K. The shift requires Liva to disclose her HR resources, or what HR objectives she relies on to run her business, and what measures she is taking to attract, retain, motivate, or develop staff. More than ever before, the value of Liva's people will boost the value of her company.

The CHRO

When 40-year-old Dennis launched his HR career in benefits 15 years ago, "Chief Human Resources Officer" wasn't a real title. HR was an afterthought, and his managers never dialogued directly with executive leadership.

But Dennis now reports to the CEO of his 55,000-person food and beverage company based in the UK. At the beginning of the pandemic, Dennis was called a hero because he successfully transitioned his workforce to a fully remote model.

Over time, the cracks started to show. Prior to Covid-19, Dennis didn't have to deal with employee growth and well-being. A lot of ground could be covered by expansive benefits like nice offices, free food and drinks, and access to a large catalog of online courses. However, with hybrid work, everything changed. Offices were not the draw, communication and collaboration became difficult, and growing attrition highlighted that merely giving access to learning catalogs was not enough to retain good employees. He had to do more, and there had to be real strategy and detail behind it.

The learning portal Dennis had been very proud of three years ago, along with several smaller talent development initiatives, could not provide proper insight into his workforce's full capabilities. And because they were rolled out ad hoc, they were misaligned with internal needs and the needs of the market. Post-pandemic, they were not resulting in an improved pipeline and were failing to provide direction in terms of upskilling and reskilling existing employees.

During Covid-19, Dennis saw how some of his employees moved seamlessly from one department to another. They had a greater ability to learn than he'd ever envisioned. Dennis is now seeing the value in hiring and promoting for potential at a larger scale, but he isn't sure where to begin to make this happen.

The employee

Twenty-nine-year-old Maria lives in Sacramento, California. She was the first in her family to go to college and now works as an accountant for a large healthcare organization. She enjoys her job and would like to stay with the company for the foreseeable future but feels at a loss when it comes to her professional development. Her manager tells her to take charge of her career, but Maria isn't sure what that means.

Maria realizes that automation will soon render many of her accounting skills obsolete. She wants to remain valuable internally and thinks she might want to explore different functional domains such as marketing or IT.

She is interested in taking courses to pursue these goals but lacks an understanding of the amount of work it will take to transition to a new area. She also doesn't know if a new position will allow her to work remotely, or if she will be at a disadvantage doing so. These are valid concerns given that Maria is married and wants to start a family soon.

Meanwhile, Maria's mother Sandra works across town as a spa franchise manager paid hourly. At 62, Sandra is a veteran of the personal care industry but in the last few decades, many things have changed. Sandra finds it hard to keep up with the new best practices and how connected operations are to technology.

Like her daughter, Sandra is eager to learn but lacks organizational guidance for how to best contribute her skills in the years before retirement. Sandra did not intend to work past 65 but lost a lot of her savings during a bout of unemployment during the pandemic. She knows that as she ages, she will need a job that doesn't require her to be on her feet 10 hours a day, but she earns good money now and doesn't want to shift to a job that will pay less.

Maria and Sandra talk often about their respective employers. Both wish their organizations would better advise them on how to

upskill, reskill, and remain relevant as their individual circumstances and the needs of their companies change.

The candidate

Damen is a 35-year-old African-American graphic designer. He has
been laid off several times over the last decade due to circumstances
outside of his control. After spending long periods unemployed and
worried about his financial welfare, Damen is burned out.

Damen has already worked in a variety of industries. In the past,
he has secured employment starting with an online application, but
as he gains additional skills and therefore has more possibilities,
he's finding this process more frustrating.

For example, when Damen goes to a company website, he is
directed to look for open positions by department. But graphic
designers are employed in many different departments and most
likely in places Damen hasn't even thought about—where should
he start? The opportunity to search by skill is not typically available. Damen can't count the number of times he has exited a career
site without completing an application.

Even when he does finish the process, Damen wonders if his
resume did the job. He didn't finish college because he couldn't
afford it and knew that graphic design certifications would give him
the skills he needed to work.

However, he believes that sometimes his application is automatically dismissed because he didn't receive a degree from a certain
university. Damen also doesn't have room on his resume to list
every design program he knows—what if a robot is weeding him
out for listing one and not another?

Right now, Damen could really use some transparency. He
doesn't know whether he is missing something in his portfolio—
if there's a skill he needs to strengthen or a better way to present
his experience. If he had this information, he could do something
about it.

And while Damen always feels a bit of excitement when he gets
called for an interview, interviews make him anxious because he

never knows where he is in the process. He might have as many as five interviews with a single company, only to assume he has been rejected when he never hears back.

Sometimes, Damen is told that the company is going with another candidate and that his resume will be kept on file for future opportunities. Damen knows no one will look at it again. He wishes he could be considered for new positions as they arise and that there was a way to update his skills for organizations with which he's interviewed or worked in the past.

In this employment market, Damen is sure to get a new job soon. But the company he signs with will most likely be the one with the most efficient recruitment process, rather than the one that's truly the best fit for him.

SPOTLIGHT ON DEXCOM
Healthcare technology company leveraged AI to improve its hiring experience for both managers and candidates.

Dexcom is a pioneer in continuous glucose monitoring solutions. Its technology helps people with diabetes keep their blood glucose levels at safe and healthy levels—without the pain or invasiveness of traditional glucose monitoring measures. The company's flagship product uses sensors to provide users with in-depth, real-time data on their blood glucose levels and uploads insights to an electronic device of choice.

To continue creating innovative products like these, Dexcom relies on dedicated, skilled employees. The company had grown significantly in the past five years, and it needed to hire a high volume of new employees across all of its recruiting segments.

However, the market for talent is extremely competitive, and Dexcom's cumbersome and time-consuming recruiting process for both applicants and decision-makers was holding the company back. Applicants had to apply "the old-fashioned way"—manually searching through open positions to find ones that seemed to fit them best.

Using a new, AI-based system, Dexcom trained bots to provide the most critical information that decision-makers need about candidates. The system also made it far easier for candidates to apply. Applicants simply

upload their resumes to the Dexcom hiring website, and AI tools
content against requirements for available positions—anywhere
organization.

"From a candidate experience perspective, it's mind-blowing," said Matt
Hill, director of talent acquisition at Dexcom. "It's a couple of clicks, and
you have not only a set of jobs that look like they fit your background, but
also descriptions of why—down to the skill level."

This shift alone resulted in a 40 percent conversion of all website
visitors to unique job applicants within six months.

Dexcom also implemented an internal mobility module that encourages
employees to upload their resumes just like external applicants. They can
match with jobs across the entire company, opening doors to opportunities
beyond their specific business unit or department.

"We support our employees when they want to move across the
company and toward their career goals," Hill told us. "Technology shouldn't
get in the way of that. It should unlock the conversations that need to
happen for our employees to grow and succeed."

The citizen

Twenty-four-year-old Elizabeth grew up in Ohio, just outside
Columbus. After graduating high school, Elizabeth took a job in
warehouse logistics for a multi-purpose e-commerce company.

In the six years since she started working, automation on the
warehouse floor has evolved significantly and global disruptions in
the supply chain mean operations are not as reliable as they once
were. But Elizabeth has learned on the fly.

Now, Elizabeth needs her company and community to help
prepare her for the next stage of her career. Her state, Ohio, wants
to be known for technology and manufacturing jobs and is offering
infrastructure and utility benefits to organizations that stay or relocate there. Although Ohio is home to several large universities,
talent is still scarce.

Elizabeth would love to stay in her home state, close to her
parents and aging grandparents. She has valuable skills in

technology oversight from which her current company and others would surely benefit.

However, because she doesn't have a college degree, Elizabeth's company is reluctant to promote her to warehousing leadership or retrain her to do something new for which she has potential but not precise experience.

If only the state of Ohio and its businesses could work together to keep talented people like Elizabeth. But as it stands, Elizabeth is considering a move. She sees a billboard about the plentiful opportunities in neighboring Indiana every time she drives on the highway and believes there may be more for her there.

The veteran

At 45, Peter has worked as an officer in the US Navy for over two decades. Throughout his tenure in the armed services, Peter has acquired excellent leadership and technology skills.

Peter's mentors have shared that civilian employers would be grateful to hire someone with such a stellar track record of motivating and developing teams and implementing new strategic initiatives.

But as he attempts to write a resume in preparation for his transition out of the Navy, Peter often finds himself staring at a blank computer screen. He doesn't understand all he has to offer the civilian world other than the obvious police and security functions, and he lacks the context to figure it out on his own.

Peter is also concerned that his history as a ranked officer will pigeonhole him as a person who leads by command and control in an ultra-hierarchical environment. He has already heard rumblings of this at the few career fairs he has attended. Employers say, "thank you for your service," and try to put him in a box based on what they think he can and cannot do.

Peter has yet to receive much positive reinforcement that his Navy skills will readily translate to a private-sector company. He sees that the government's transition assistance program is trying its best, but there is still no clear path.

Across the board, Peter's transition is filled with anxiety. Not only does he need a new job, but he has to learn the ins and outs of life in civilian society. And the day-to-day support he received in the Navy is soon to be a thing of the past.

In his ideal world, Peter and his wife would settle in a low-key suburb of Washington, D.C., while Peter "tries out" different job functions as part of a company apprenticeship program. He is interested in both business development and project management.

If a company would be willing to invest time and training in Peter as he explores post-Navy career options available to him in the market, that company might have a loyal and versatile employee for life.

Fortunately, technology can assist us in solving both the individual and collective challenges faced by Peter and our other members of the workforce. Now that you better understand the macrotrends—from talent supply mismatches to government regulation and compliance—that are shaping the development of new workforce management systems, let's use the next chapter to explore the potential of deep learning in the talent space.

APPLY THE AI

Imagine that you are the CHRO for FutureStrong, a telecommunications company with 90,000 employees that wants to take advantage of digital transformation to enter new markets.

FutureStrong is experiencing major voluntary turnover in its central IT department. The company's compensation is competitive, but it doesn't seem to matter. The average tenure is less than a year.

How might you apply this chapter's 2023 talent macrotrends (for example, focus on employee experience and flexibility, and employee listening) to hold on to these highly skilled and in-demand workers? Write your ideas here.

Chapter summary

- The **demand for skilled workers** is growing rapidly, with seven in ten employers globally saying they are struggling to find workers with the **right mix of technical skills and human capabilities**, and that there are approximately half as many available workers per open position compared with a historical 20-year average.

- Considering that much of this burnout is a direct result of juggling inflexible work with parenting schedules, nearly five million cases of it are viewed as "preventable." And only some organizations have answered their employees' calls for help.

- Hybrid work has pushed an agenda that workforce futurists have mulled for more than a decade: the need to **redesign jobs** so they align with **digital transformation**.

- Companies are making progress customizing their **employee experiences** to different groups depending on their unique journeys and requirements. The 2023 employee experience focuses on two overarching themes: **purpose and flexibility**.

- **HR compliance** has risen to a never-before-seen level of complexity. While more than 2,000 **legislative updates** related to Covid-19 streamed in across the globe, employers struggled to keep up with the policies they needed to update or create.

- Macrotrends are based on general sentiment, but sometimes research alone makes it difficult to see talent issues from all relevant angles. By telling the stories of individuals experiencing today's workforce through a variety of lenses, we can add color and meaning to the challenges we must, at the end of the day, address as a team.

2

The role of deep learning in talent

At the beginning of the Covid-19 pandemic, just as we were all getting ready to lock down, Eightfold received an inquiry from global consulting firm McKinsey. Could we adapt our software to move available workers to organizations that needed them?

Well, of course we could. Within a few hours, we'd assembled a team across three continents and had our Talent Exchange launched within two months.

While the World Health Organization was telling us to flatten the disease curve, we were flattening the unemployment curve by working with individuals, associations, universities, and companies like Starbucks, Amazon, Hyatt, Walmart, Postmates, and United Airlines to post jobs and offer up willing employees. The jobs spanned 6,000 cities across the US and Canada.

Joshua was one of our first Talent Network beneficiaries. He was working at a Starbucks in Philadelphia when he got hit with an employment double whammy. First, Joshua's hours were reduced. Then, his store was closed indefinitely. When Starbucks shared the Talent Network with Joshua and his coworkers, Joshua created a profile and quickly found a handful of appropriate jobs. He applied to Walgreens, heard back in two days, and within a week had started onboarding into a managerial role.

How was the Talent Network able to operate so efficiently in Joshua's case? It starts with data. There has been a huge amount of data generated over the last 10–15 years. In fact, most of the data in the world was created over the last two years. The Cloud introduced that data at scale, and advances in AI are allowing us to crunch that data at scale and find people like Joshua meaningful employment.

For example, take a regular coffee mug. At one time, a computer could recognize a coffee mug unless it was shaped unusually, different from other mugs. Now, technology can store information about an almost infinite number of mugs. AI can take this massive amount of data and learn that the whimsical mug shaped like the Eiffel Tower you bought on a road trip is... a mug.

You know, of course, that artificial intelligence isn't new. Netflix uses it to recommend your next movie selection, Toyota uses it to help you park and switch lanes. AI is new, however, as it pertains to talent.

In the last chapter, we talked about how the workforce is evolving as well as the perspectives of the different individuals involved in the talent process. Now, we'll address why we need artificial intelligence as our next step, and the variety of ways deep learning can power talent functions across the employee lifecycle.

All workforce data isn't created equal

In current hiring processes, we rely heavily on resumes, which haven't materially changed since Leonardo da Vinci wrote his in 1482. Resumes are error-prone because humans are inherently bad at self-assessment. And when candidates tailor their resumes to match job descriptions, they are full of platitudes, exaggerations, and omissions (people's best work and attributes are sometimes not even included) as candidates distill years of work down to a few bullet points.

Another concern is the timeliness of information. Employees update information about themselves infrequently. A person at a job for several years may not have an updated online resume or LinkedIn profile, and if they do, it probably captures only a fraction of what they have done, are doing, and are capable of doing.

Employees who have successfully worked with an organization in the past are a terrific source of talent, but unfortunately, most companies are unaware of the skills their alumni have gained since departing. Similarly, past applicants to a company could years later make great hires, but companies have no visibility into how their skills and capabilities have improved in the intervening years. Instead, recruiters tend to resort to conventional wisdom that any past rejected candidate or former employee can never be a future hire.

The overall lack of descriptive, meaningful data means employers can be negatively influenced by details with little predictive insight into a candidate's ability to excel in the job. For instance, typos, font choice, and resume layout may influence the employer's perception of the candidate's capabilities.

Historically, workforce data has also been reactive rather than proactive. Companies struggle to determine how many permanent and contingent employees they have, let alone the skills, capabilities, and potential of their workforce.

It's an even larger challenge to determine such things as: Where shall we set up our next location, based on the availability, cost, and competition for talent? What capabilities do we need for the businesses we want to be in next year, and how does this need compare to our current capabilities?

Finally, there's the untapped potential of skills adjacency, which refers to the inference that a person good at skill A often excels at skill B. For example, we can infer that someone who excels in calculus likely also excels at algebra, or we could guess that an experienced enterprise sales representative could quickly learn enterprise partnerships.

But with nearly two million unique skills globally, it is impossible for a human to understand all of them individually, the relationship between them, and the interactive role brand new skillsets will play. A human manager may review the narrow data at their disposal and then supplement it with their own perceptions and understanding of the underlying skills required to perform in a job.

For example, when a company is hiring for a customer service manager, a recruiter may search for candidates who have held that exact title or a related title. We simply have not had the tools to surface candidates who may have the right customer skills based on their work experiences.

A customer service representative at a department store may have a skill set that's more similar to a real estate agent than a customer service representative at a bank. A middle school teacher may have more of the skills required to be a fantastic product trainer at a technology company than a product operations associate already in the tech industry.

The way we've collected and analyzed skills data to date has made it difficult to break out of the traditional approach to talent acquisition, development, and management.

The deep opportunity of deep learning

The AI software market is growing at 154 percent annually, and within the next few years AI will be embedded in every industry and business process from health to education to transportation (González, 2020). Human resources is no exception, and used effectively, AI can address the workforce challenges we've been talking about. But first, we must understand what AI is and what it is not.

As with most good buzzwords, AI suffers from misuse. Companies often incorrectly claim they use AI when they simply use keyword matching and Boolean logic.

Alternatively, organizations may use pre-built decision trees and present them as AI. Such technologies may appear intelligent in that they can provide the information a human is looking for, but they lack the relevance, scale, and adaptability of true artificial intelligence.

Even when organizations do try to use AI to make decisions about who to attract, hire, upskill, retain, and rehire, their data sources are far too limited, and this often results in biased output. For example, analyzing 'successful' profiles in just your company's workforce as a model for future hires could invite historical biases that favor certain demographic groups into your process.

The most advanced form of AI involves deep learning. Deep learning is a type of machine learning inspired by the human brain. Deep learning algorithms mimic human conclusions by continuously analyzing data with a given logical structure. This structure encompasses multiple layers of algorithms called neural networks.

Deep learning algorithms can't predict the future or give answers that a human would agree with 100 percent. Yet they are still extraordinarily valuable. If you've ever used a modern search engine and been amazed by the results or if you've ever watched the perfect show recommended by your streaming network of choice, you have experienced the power of deep learning.

The main challenge of deep learning is data—specifically, the massive amount required. The talent space alone needs billions of data points about people, career trajectories, skills, and experiences.

But while AI's reach was once limited by computing power and the availability of data, that's no longer the case. Today, global neural nets can identify more than a million skills across the world's 7.8 billion people.

Then, using this data, AI engineers can develop deep learning algorithms to determine the best answers to a defined class of questions. In the case of talent, such questions might include: Who is the best fit for this specific job requirement? What job is this individual most likely to hold next in their career?

Understanding deep learning's ability to harness a massive amount of data is only the first step, however. The more important question is how deep learning can be applied to various talent processes. There are multiple answers. Let's start with talent acquisition.

Skills adjacency

As we mentioned earlier, skills adjacency refers to the inference that a person good at skill A often excels at skill B, and when we can understand it fully, it helps us complete our picture of a human's true potential and the transferable skills they possess.

"This (skills adjacency) could be a way of opening non-traditional pathways for candidates who don't have the experience doing the exact job needed but have every ounce of capability required," said Jolen Anderson, the global head of human resources for BNY Mellon.

For the last decade, the global economy has been in flux. For instance, frontline healthcare workers have worked in very stressful conditions throughout the pandemic years, and churn is high. Hospitals are losing nurses—not to other hospitals, but to the now rebounding hospitality industry. This is because the skills that nurses have in abundance—attention to detail, responsiveness, digital literacy, and a caring approach—are also very relevant to a hospitality business. And the stress level is much lower!

As a personal example, Nico Iannotti is Eightfold's top sales engineer in Europe, but he wasn't always involved with either sales or technology. He was, however, previously involved with customer service as a sommelier and waiter. As he put it, skills are interchangeable assets that individuals can leverage in a variety of industry roles and life situations.

"Many of the skills I acquired prior to my corporate career have been very helpful in my role as a client relationship manager and solution engineer." He told us: "What is the link between pairing wines and selling software? Both are customer-facing roles and both provide solutions to a customer's problem. In both cases, you are building relationships, demonstrating empathy, and selling an emotional experience based on a specific budget. In both roles, when a customer complains, you have to respond and make a decision in the moment. Whether you are recommending a croissant, a white wine, or software, the customer has to believe you have the expertise to be a trusted adviser. It's just a change of context, not a completely different skill set."

Deep learning can break down human work experience into capabilities and match those capabilities with jobs available now. For example, many like Iannotti have found work in corporate jobs, and a major bank told us that many new employees were formerly bartenders. This isn't an association one would readily make!

Similarly, if a company is looking for project management skills, resumes and job descriptions often fail to surface the right matches. But deep learning can tell us that a candidate or employee's skills are validated or likely based on their work experience, even if the person never had a title called 'project manager' or listed 'project management' as a skill on their resume. On the flip side, deep learning can determine if a candidate for a project management job is missing the required skills despite a prior project management title.

In other words, deep learning calls out potential by looking at people with similar skills and what they were able to accomplish next in their career. Thanks to a global data set in which you can analyze thousands of people who acquired new skills and were subsequently successful in a new role, you can infer that a fresh candidate can also learn these skills and do well in this new role.

Why is it important that technology tells us what people are capable of versus what they can do today? A company might ask for three years of Android development experience in a job advertisement, for example, but could you do the job if you had two years of Android experience and a few years of IoS experience? Likely yes. Deep learning can help us get to the heart of what's actually needed in a role, not what we assume.

Understanding potential is highly important to employers because it allows them to be much more flexible about how they can deploy talented and loyal workers as business demands change. It also assists with diversity challenges. What if, for the sake of argument, people who have multiple years of Android experience skew heavily toward one group, such as men, but women have more IoS experience and can do the Android job just as well?

Let's dive deeper into how this analysis of potential plays out. Imagine that three people have worked as product managers. One of them worked at Google, one worked at Honeywell, and one at Delta Airlines. A deep learning system knows, with a high degree of certainty, that the person from Honeywell has skills that the Delta and Google people do not. It can also tell whether the Delta and Google product managers could easily learn the skills the Honeywell person has, and how they could go about doing so.

Huggy Rao, a professor of organizational behavior and human resources at the Stanford University School of Business, described a conversation with a successful Stanford graduate who rose quickly in the world of finance. "The graduate said they owe most of their jobs not to hard skills but to trust. They wouldn't have been able to do the work with the skills they had on Day 1. But employers trusted that they could learn."

The use of deep learning means that this type of trust isn't based on blind faith but rather on a comprehensive analysis.

SPOTLIGHT ON CHEVRON

Oil and gas giant combined a rich existing data set with the power of deep learning to extract key insights about essential worker skills.

Chevron had a treasure trove of HR data at its disposal, but Julie Flowers, head of global talent acquisition, wasn't sure how to best use it. Chevron had a variety of complex and overlapping systems that made it difficult to find the right talent both inside and outside the organization.

As Flowers shared in a session at the HR Technology conference and later with Phil Albinus on *HRExecutive.com*: "We've been focused on having that right talent in the right place with the right skill set at the right time" (Albinus, 2021).

Her first challenge, according to the session, was making sense of the carefully stored data inside Chevron's HR systems so that the recruitment team could more effectively review resumes and applications from external and internal candidates.

Chevron decided to set up a deep learning platform with the goal of aggregating and extracting insights from the data it had and understanding the skills that candidates and employees have.

Deep learning helps Chevron's recruitment team assess whether a given applicant meets the job's requirements or if they would be better suited for another role in the organization. As a result, the recruiters themselves have become superhuman talent experts.

"We transformed our traditional recruiters into career advisers because now we don't need to spend as much time making sure the fit is there," Luis Niño, a member of Flowers' HR team, told Albinus at *HRExecutive.com*. "The platform has provided us with algorithms that make correlations, inferences, and adjacencies to match the right candidate to the right job."

Niño offered the example of agility, sharing that based on the algorithmic results, he can assess a candidate's aperture for learning and their ability to transfer their skills to another space. "This is a game changer when it comes to evaluating potential."

The new technology helps hiring managers too. "We can source talent and recruit talent internally at a much more rapid speed and with better quality," Flowers said.

Candidate experience

In the HR world, we like to talk about candidate experience, and when we do, we usually discuss things like improving corporate career websites, giving feedback to job candidates not hired, and speeding up the hiring process. Unfortunately, despite our efforts, application rates are still low.

Why is this happening? Well, when candidates search for a job on a career website, they often can't find a job that exactly matches their skills and don't feel they even have a chance at an interview.

As an example, some career sites ask candidates to begin their search by choosing a department within the company. Many times, the candidate doesn't know where to start because companies tend to use different words to describe the same function.

Even assuming the candidate could guess the right department, many career sites try to match them based on a title and what they're doing now. The technology doesn't look at the skills that could be redeployed elsewhere for a different type of job.

Posted job descriptions can be a barrier too, especially when it comes to applicant diversity. A well-publicized study from Hewlett-Packard found that women are more likely than men to opt out of applying for a job if they don't meet 100 percent of the qualifications (Youn, 2019).

Deep learning can go a long way in preventing the drop-off between search and application. First off, such a platform can offer immediate personalization. Many organizations have spent a great deal of money on branding and designing career sites and then advertising them, but when a candidate gets to the site, the content is undifferentiated.

In other words, the entry-level job seeker looking for a job at a restaurant chain sees similar content to an attorney looking to be that chain's in-house counsel. Deep learning can show candidates content that relates specifically to them in the form of videos, blog posts, or employee introductions.

If a candidate uploads a resume to the company's website, deep learning can compare that applicant's skills with the skills required for each of the company's roles. The resulting report illustrates to the candidate that they are indeed a fit, and they are more likely to go through with an application.

Let's envision that a software engineer at a large healthcare company uploads their resume to a career website powered by deep learning. The system actually knows a great deal about their skills, whether they were listed in the resume or not. The technology has this information because it has examined millions of profiles of people with similar experience. It can compare the skills that this software engineer has with the skills that someone with the same title at another healthcare company has.

For example, deep learning can quickly learn a business, understanding that a customer service candidate at one coffee chain or retailer is different from a customer service candidate at another chain. It can know that a product manager at one company is more technical or more business-oriented than a product manager at a competitor company. The system has analyzed so much data and seen so many career paths that it knows what skills are used in various departments of different companies.

It can also update a candidate's profile with data from hundreds of public data sources such as LinkedIn and Google. Going back to the example of the software engineer at the healthcare company, even if the word "multitasker" is never mentioned in the candidate's application materials, deep learning might determine that the candidate is indeed a great multitasker simply by knowing their name, title, and company.

Deep learning can also take individuals whose capabilities are difficult to translate and match them with available jobs. One of our favorite examples, and one that you'll hear a lot more about in Chapter 5, involves the transition of veterans to the civilian workforce. An infantry sergeant has experience boosting morale and working with teams, as well as skills in influencing and listening. This person could be a great salesperson in a Fortune 500 company, and deep learning can help us recognize this instead of moving right along because a military title doesn't line up exactly with a business one.

Phil Dana is the chief human resources officer at Asklepios BioPharmaceutical, a biotechnology company, and a Naval Academy graduate. As a longtime supporter of veterans, he told us:

> I have always strongly championed veterans in HR positions to capitalize on their knowledge of talent. But the title doesn't readily translate. If you look at most of the senior HR leaders who are also veterans, hardly any of them were human resources professionals in the military. I'm excited that AI is uncovering veterans' true strengths and pairing them with career paths they (and we) might not have thought about.

Candidate journeys and performance

Deep learning can uncover trends in employee journeys the way humans simply cannot. For example, after people leave sales roles at a certain company, do we keep track of what they did next? Up until recently, we couldn't. But now, we can predict the next moves of a future salesperson at that company.

Better yet, deep learning can capture the dimension of time. A human recruiter, seeing General Electric on a candidate's resume, may think 'GE is a good company to have worked for' without any further understanding. But deep learning can tell us why working in a certain job in a certain team or department of GE during a certain time period is more (or less) valuable.

The way AI sees time helps explain the difference between AI and "skills libraries" or other attempts at organizing skills. Earlier, we talked about how these systems understand the difference between three people with the same title but who worked at Google, Honeywell, and Delta Airlines.

The time factor allows us to go beyond this. Deep learning can tell us that someone who held a job with one title at a company learned and accomplished different things than the person who held that job at the same company a decade prior. Same idea with schools. Deep learning can tell us that a person with a degree from a given university learned different material than a person with the same major during a different time period. All these variations lead to different career paths: one job or one degree might be better preparation for a specific career than that job or degree at another time.

Stanford professor Huggy Rao said this time element is not examined nearly enough. "Everyone is going to succeed. And everyone, at some point, is going to fail. But how do you respond?" he asked. "You did a certain thing when the economy was great. How can we know if that was you, or the tailwinds of the macroeconomic forces? How can you normalize this data to understand what great performance looks like in a sour economy?"

Deep learning can also help us avoid taking certain performance data out of context. For instance, a hospital chain might automatically assume that a doctor with great patient outcomes is better than one with so-so outcomes. But patient outcomes are a limited measure. What if the first doctor works in a far more affluent area with far healthier patients?

Similarly, a high school teacher with students who then go on to college 90 percent of the time isn't necessarily better than one whose students attend college 50 percent of the time. College attendance as a measure of teacher quality depends on the area they teach in. Deep learning can suss out these nuances.

Of course, humans have played and will continue to play a critical role in the talent acquisition process. But deep learning adds value to this process by essentially making every candidate or employee profile dynamic. Every person who engages with your organization is accumulating a trail of skills and experience: interview notes, performance reviews, social media footprints, online videos, and so on. Deep learning applies these details for a more multidimensional, real-time view of the person—helping us to avoid bias. Preventing bias is a topic we will explore a great deal throughout this book, particularly as it pertains to our pursuit of stronger diversity, inclusion, and belonging.

As another example, some candidates take career breaks for reasons unrelated to their professional lives, such as elder or childcare. By using deep learning to understand why career breaks happen, organizations can potentially recalibrate their requirements rather than unceremoniously dismissing these candidates with breaks.

Candidate marketing

Most organizations have a ton of past applicants who've all been told "we'll keep your resume on file and get back to you if there's an appropriate opportunity." But do companies actually get back to people? Not usually, even if a candidate was a valuable employee referral or someone who was the second choice for a job offer. We also tend to immediately forget our most talented alumni when, knowing how fluid employment is today, they should be at the top of our pipeline.

Deep learning interfaces with candidate relationship management technology to send prospective candidates email with content targeted to them. Depending on the audience segment (for example, recent college graduates or mid-level managers in the Northeast), this might include volunteer work the company is doing, stories about employees who got great promotions, or patents the company earned.

You can even set your deep learning platform to review marketing content on your company website—like press releases or blog posts— and automatically build an email campaign to share it with the prospective candidates who'd be most interested in the subject matter.

SPOTLIGHT ON NUTANIX

Software firm used deep learning to find and target communication to passive candidates and past applicants.

Nutanix is a global leader in cloud software, and a pioneer in helping enterprise customers manage apps in private, hybrid, and multi-cloud environments. The company already employs more than 6,000 people and is looking for new technical talent all the time. Unfortunately, these "purple squirrels" (or individuals with rare and highly sought-after skills) often prove elusive.

"These are the proverbial passive candidates," recruiter Chanda Townsend told us. "They are employed, have plenty of options, and don't always respond to recruiters. And, LinkedIn has limited capability for customization."

By adopting deep learning, Nutanix now has an alternative to sending out cold emails to disinterested prospects. The outreach process uses a combination of human and machine intelligence. When a hiring manager and recruiter open up a requisition, they calibrate the role so the system understands what's needed to do the job successfully. This can include inputting "ideal" candidate profiles, or high performers doing the job today. Then, the platform reviews past applicants, past employees, employee referrals, and newly sourced or passive applicants to stack rank individuals as strong matches.

Through this system of calibration, Nutanix can see how different requirements shrink or expand candidate pool diversity and ask whether a given requirement is necessary. For instance, will the company get more diverse applicants if recruiters remove the four-year degree requirement?

In another major moment of insight, Nutanix also realized that some of the best applicants were people with whom the company already engaged. "We find a lot of great candidates among silver medalists," Townsend shared. "These are the people who were high in consideration for other roles, and for whatever reason we had gone with someone else."

A deep learning platform rediscovers these past applicants, enriching their profiles with skills and experience they've gained since the initial interview.

"A req should never start from zero," Townsend told us. "You should always have a pool of candidates to whom you can send personalized communication."

At Nutanix, recruiters and hiring managers work together to tag and bucket prospects based on the skills needed, and to build out the messaging for each bucket. As an example, Nutanix might focus on women engineers and send them an email inviting them to an exclusive event with the company's CTO. Open rates for these communications are as high as 70 percent. And even if a prospect says they aren't looking for a new job right now, the system keeps them warm with periodic, customized outreach.

Workforce management

We've talked a lot about talent acquisition in this chapter, but deep learning can have a substantial impact on other HR functions including contingent worker management and internal mobility and skills gaps reductions.

Contingent/contract worker management

The gig economy has grown by around 30 percent in the last few years, and according to ADP, about one in six workers is doing contract, temporary, gig, seasonal, or other contingent work for an organization (Yildirmaz et al, 2020).

To stay competitive in the fight for workers, leaders must be proactive in staying connected with those who could potentially meet their staffing needs.

Using contingent workers, contract workers, or freelancers makes sense for several reasons. There's the obvious fact that these workers don't require the amount of overhead and benefits of full-time employees and therefore are a viable option for growing your organization in manageable increments.

In most cases, contingent workers also come pre-skilled, having been responsible for professional development on their own time. This comes in handy, especially when it comes to quickly outdated technical skills that you might not need from a full-time employee in five years.

We love the story of construction startup Modern Cube Modular Homes, which builds homes from recycled shipping containers and high-rise materials. "There's no way a startup company like us could afford to bring on a huge full-time crew," founder Baron Christopher Hanson told Matt Alderton at *Redshift by Autodesk*. "We've been able to bring on those experts on a part-time or an as-needed basis to work on whatever projects we're building" (Alderton, 2019).

Contingent workers also grant organizations access to a larger pool of workers, including caregivers who can't work a traditional 9–5 job. Let's say that a large, far-flung company is looking for someone who speaks Portuguese and also has web development skills. It's likely that someone in the company's contingent work-force has the right combination, but it's also very possible that the hiring manager won't readily identify this person.

Deep learning allows organizations to capture the complete capabilities of an organization's contingent workforce and readily deploy workers on projects. It updates contingent worker profiles automatically so that hiring managers can understand the skills and experience that workers may have added since their last stint with the company.

Then, there's the benefit of predictive analytics, a function of AI that provides insights into future hiring needs and suggests contingent workers accordingly.

When you manage your contingent workforce this way, you can provide a personal touch yourself, rather than leaving relationships in the hands of outside vendors. More frequent and meaningful engagement also increases contingent worker job security and therefore company loyalty.

This is a significant benefit when you think about how most contract work operates today. People come and go and the knowledge and experience are lost. You may decide you want an amazing contingent worker back, but you can't talk to them directly because your relationship was with a third-party company rather than with the worker.

You *want* ready access to your past contract workers because we estimate that bringing back someone you've used before can result in a 40–60 percent drop in both hiring costs and hiring time for an open position.

Internal mobility

As we know, turnover is expensive, costing businesses alone nearly $1 trillion annually. Voluntary turnover in 2021 was as high as 25 percent (U.S. Bureau of Labor Statistics, 2021). We often think that turnover costs and hiring costs are one and the same, but there's more to it. The loss of knowledge and customer relationships can hurt too.

We tell employees to drive their own careers, but how can they do that when they don't understand what it takes to get a more appropriate job in another department or location?

At most organizations, internal mobility is limited to posting jobs in-house (which most people don't see) before sourcing from the outside. But especially in large organizations where matches across departmental lines are less evident, the path to a desirable internal move is unclear.

This is too bad because people often quit for new challenges, and sometimes those people who quit might have found those challenges in the form of open jobs in their own companies!

Deep learning can solve this easily. It breaks down a person's profile and history into skills, suggesting how the company might redeploy those skills. It can prompt a hiring manager to think, "This may be the job they do well, but is there a way to put their skills to work for us elsewhere?" If they have an open requisition, deep learning can show them if there's a matching employee within the company—perhaps in a division the manager never thought about.

Deep learning can further distill individual employee skills and experience into capabilities and encourage curious employees to view internal roles that are a match for those capabilities. Maybe the new role is appropriate now, or perhaps it's aspirational. If the latter, deep learning can guide employees in pursuing coursework or training to prepare sufficiently for that role.

Let's say an employee sees an internal role open in the finance department. Deep learning sees that their skills are a good match but they'd be a stronger match if they took a tax-related course unique to that company's industry. That employee then knows how to move from job A to job B, and even find the right course in the company's learning management system.

Or, let's suppose there is no open role but a lower-level designer wants to become a design director in their company. This employee can examine the paths other design employees took to get to the director role, including the skills and characteristics design directors have and the coursework that they have taken. The employee then has the option to connect to the learning management system and sign up for classes to help them move from designer to director.

Deep learning also identifies flight risks. It'll tell you how long an employee has been in a certain role and assess whether that person might be itching to move on. Organizations using deep learning don't have to wait for the exit interview to determine that an employee quit because their career had stalled. They can preempt this by proactively redeploying this employee to meet a new challenge both for themselves and for the company.

Workforce and skills gaps reductions

If you have a workforce full of capable and loyal employees, it seems senseless to lay off thousands of them because one group is struggling while simultaneously hiring thousands of external (and therefore unknown) people in another group that's growing.

Workforce reductions aren't good for your reputation either. The CEO of the mortgage lender Better.com, Vishal Garg, is just one example of an executive coming under fire for a layoff. After letting go 9 percent of his workforce (900 employees, many of whom didn't have poor performance) on a Zoom call, Garg received global and largely unfavorable media coverage that will affect his business and career for a long time to come.

Deep learning can save jobs and keep your organization in good public stead by providing a blueprint to place employees/people? In relevant internal positions where their capabilities are a fit.

On the other side of the equation, critical workforce skills gaps plague many mid-21st-century organizations, and yet most do not understand the scale of the problem, where the gaps are exactly, and how much these gaps could impact future growth.

Let's take the example of a global consumer packaged goods company that specializes in snack foods. Many of its competitors are starting to offer nutritious, fresh, and plant-based foods, and if our company wants to keep up, it needs to align its workforce's skills with this reality. Deep learning can give a company visibility into what capabilities are needed to prepare, what gaps exist in its current workforce, how its capabilities compare to the capabilities of its competitors, and how organizational learning programs can get up to speed. Don't worry, we'll explore these topics more in Chapter 4!

We've now covered how deep learning can power a variety of functions across the employee lifecycle. In particular, we've talked extensively about the role deep learning can play in improving the efficiency of your talent acquisition and management. In the next chapter, we will peek under the hood to understand how you can deploy a talent intelligence platform to achieve all the benefits we just described.

APPLY THE AI

Returning to our example of the FutureStrong company, envision that FutureStrong is experiencing a shortage of call center professionals in its New York office. Even after increasing the pay, the organization is not receiving enough applications for open roles by searching for call center experience in local LinkedIn profiles.

How might FutureStrong use this chapter's deep learning strategies for both talent acquisition and internal mobility to uncover non-traditional call center candidates? For instance, it recruiters might consider candidates with skills adjacencies rather than straightforward call center expertise. Write your ideas here.

Chapter summary

- The **lack of descriptive, meaningful data** in most resumes means employers can be negatively influenced by details with **little predictive insight** into a candidate's ability to excel in the job. For instance, typos, font choice, and resume layout may influence the employer's perception of the candidate's capabilities.

- Some talent applications may appear intelligent, but they lack the sensitivity, scale, and adaptability of **deep learning**. When organizations use these to make decisions about who to attract, hire, upskill, retain, and rehire, their **data sources are far too limited,** and this often results in biased output.

- Using deep learning to assess **skills adjacency** opens non-traditional pathways for candidates who don't have the experience doing the exact job needed but have every ounce of capability required.

- Deep learning can quickly learn the specifics of an individual business. These platforms have analyzed so much data and seen so many **career paths** that they know the skills used in various departments of different companies. They can also round out candidate profiles with data from hundreds of **public data sources.**

- Via deep learning, an organization can capture the complete capabilities of its **contingent workforce** and readily deploy workers on projects. Deep learning updates contingent worker profiles automatically so that hiring managers can understand the skills and experience that workers may have added since their last stint with the company.

- The path to a desirable internal move is unclear, especially in large organizations where matches across departmental lines are less evident. Deep learning breaks down a person's profile and history into skills, suggesting how the company might **redeploy those skills.** It can also analyze an individual employee's profile to encourage them to view internal roles that are a match for their capabilities.

3

Under the hood of talent intelligence

We've all heard about companies getting rid of the bottom 5–10 percent of their employees on a regular basis. It's the "GE mantra" after all. But here's the key element: how did they select the bottom performers?

We know that 70–80 percent of people apply to the wrong jobs, get hired into roles that are not the best fit for them, and then soldier on through the work without loving or even liking it. They eventually part ways with the company.

As we learn more about what a person is capable of doing, understanding the roles we need performed provides the context for the employees or candidates. Both hiring managers and individuals must understand who is a strong fit and why. In today's world, when jobs are changing rapidly and people have varied and colorful career trajectories, it's even more important that role requirements keep pace.

Deep learning can help us guide people to new career paths they hadn't even considered. We recall a panel of journalists talking about what they did after they lost their jobs. One person became a career counselor. Another became a policeman. These seemed like odd transitions at first, but the former journalists explained that all of these jobs involve asking questions and being good listeners. AI can spot trends like this where humans cannot.

These are the insights that led Ashu and Eightfold's CTO Varun Kacholia to build a deep learning platform that could assess both people (what they have done and what they are capable of doing) and the roles they are expected to perform. Deep learning can help us make this information more precise, leading to recommendations that are transparent to and build trust and confidence on both sides. It's this formula that leads to greater diversity in hiring, including more women, Black Americans, and veterans.

The question you are probably asking—and rightfully so—is how does it work? We might say that deep learning can do all these things in hiring and the rest of the talent lifecycle, but what does that look like from a technology perspective?

The deep learning approach to talent we described in the last chapter is based heavily on talent intelligence, which defines roles and uses internal company data as well as external, local, and global data to help decision-makers optimize talent decisions.

Talent intelligence dynamically self-learns until it fully understands the availability, maturity, relevance, learnability, and evolution of skills within specific organizations and the larger market. Its resulting analyses provide leaders with complete visibility into the skills of their existing workforce and the training and hiring required to keep pace with industry developments.

In this chapter, we'll touch upon how talent intelligence helps in redesigning job architecture, how it works with your data to provide multidimensional insights into hiring decisions, and how to access the benefits of talent intelligence in a single platform.

Redesigning job architectures

According to our partner Josh Bersin, one of the most devilish problems in business is building and revising a job architecture (Bersin, 2021).

"Consider the enormous transformations taking place in the economy. Jobs are automated, enhanced, and changed by technology daily," he said. "Companies are moving into new business models, people are working in agile teams, and remote employees operate under substantially less supervision. How do you design your jobs lattice so it makes sense and is efficient and up to date?"

And, when you recruit, promote, or move people from role to role, how do you define the job requirements, the skills needed, the levels, and the pay?

A job architecture that's clear and simple is the backbone of talent intelligence. "Companies are like your drawers at home in that they get more cluttered over time. Every time a manager hires someone, they create a job and a rough list of responsibilities for that role," Bersin said. "Before you know it, your company has 20 different job titles equating to 'analyst,' and dozens of 'project managers' scattered across the company."

Bersin recalled talking with the engineering department at Yelp. The group had database engineers (back end), application developers (mid-tier), front-end developers (user interface), designers, and even "full-stack" engineers (who could work with the entire product).

As Bersin noted, overly complex job architectures cause problems, including failing to keep track of the multitude of people doing the same thing in different places and the inability to create a global skills inventory. After all, who can tell what people know when everyone has their own customized job title?

There are also challenges with pay equity and job mobility. One technology company told Bersin that talent mobility is stalled because "nobody will take a new position unless they get a promotion." The company had 65 different levels!

As for Yelp's engineering team, its leadership gave up trying to make sense of all this. "Eventually, the company decided to simply call everyone an engineer. Sure, they have various levels and responsibilities, but the job titles are totally fungible, and management can move people around without all these headaches."

Once you've simplified your roles as much as possible, you'll want to consolidate them into professional capability groups. We talked with Bersin about what this means.

Roles like engineering, marketing, sales, and even HR have professional capabilities and these capabilities should be clearly defined and owned by a capability leader in the company.

"The capability leader is responsible for keeping track of the skills and technologies people really need, and then making sure all the circles of people in that functional area (who may report to other groups) know where they fit in the career model," Bersin told us.

The capability leader is typically a seasoned expert or professional who knows the function and can sponsor skills and career programs in the domain via "Capability Academies."

If you haven't outlined your professional capabilities and don't have capability leaders governing your functional areas yet, you might want to think about your job architecture redesign from a fresh perspective. You will need a leader, team, and process to do this well.

In putting together your job architecture team and process, recognize that job architecture impacts everything. "Recruiters will test the system as they search for candidates and see new job titles in the market. The compensation team will want data on job levels and new hybrid job roles that impact your design," said Bersin.

"L&D teams will use the job architecture for onboarding, development, and career planning. And every manager needs this information so they can efficiently set up their teams and then hire, manage, and reward people."

Your company too will need a "Job Architect," or as Bersin suggested, a "Head of Skills Architecture." Ideally, this leader will have a substantial HR background with experience in other functional areas as well, and a team to support them.

Verizon is going through a job architecture simplification process now. The company has put into place a functional team tasked with refreshing the job architecture on a regular basis, assigning circle owners to own each functional area, and developing a series of capability academies to ensure each functional area stays current on skills, technologies, and careers.

Bersin suggested that reconfiguring job architectures is an opportunity for innovation. "While you may want to be industry standard in your roles and jobs, this is actually an opportunity to push the envelope," he said. "If you're a consumer goods company, for example, you may want to organize your go-to-market business around customer age or demographic. This strategy could create a new family of jobs (for example, Generation X marketing lead)."

Introducing talent intelligence

For the capability leader, locating the related skills within the organization and synthesizing expertise are no small feats. This is where talent intelligence technology comes into play.

Talent intelligence allows the capability leader to examine all the jobs in the world pertaining to a given function and determine who in the organization is doing roughly the same thing under a different job title.

Our client BNY Mellon, for example, used talent intelligence to consolidate 3,000 IT and operations jobs in six to eight weeks using this system and is now planning on consolidating all 31,000 jobs by year-end.

But how is this done exactly?

In the last chapter, we talked about uncovering skills adjacencies. Talent intelligence examines skill adjacency and context to determine current organizational capabilities and future needs. It also provides a consistent and unbiased evaluation of individual capabilities against globally standardized job descriptions and requirements.

That journey begins with an assessment of the as-is workforce. The talent intelligence platform ingests current jobs and skills taxonomies to provide assessment of job descriptions and their associated skill sets. It identifies duplicate positions and provides clearer roles and responsibilities as well as guidance for placement within specific teams or divisions.

The platform refines existing skills from a skills requirement perspective, modifying descriptions to identify skill sets, education, and professional backgrounds needed to successfully fill the role. It also calls out position gaps and places new roles within the organizational hierarchy to be filled either internally or externally.

The assessment process, undertaken by HR and/or the capability leaders, is guided by an AI assistant. The interface assistant walks the leader through their decision making, using machine learning to provide insightful recommendations that align with the organization's identified job responsibilities and global benchmarks for like positions.

After the initial assessment, the talent intelligence platform offers long-term strategic recommendations for skills and positions that may not be needed now but are indicated in the organization's short- or long-term plans.

Following the alignment phase, the platform builds a jobs library—an easy-access repository of roles and descriptions for recruiters and business leaders to quickly populate organizational design layouts.

Once an initial jobs taxonomy has been set up and tested, the talent intelligence platform automatically provides updated recommendations as internal and external circumstances evolve.

Using talent intelligence technology to underpin your job architecture redesign will result in increased transparency of current jobs and skills requirements. This may lead you to move current employees to new divisions, optimize your teams for greater productivity, or upskill and reskill employees via integration with your learning management system.

Talent intelligence also provides increased confidence in succession planning, helping you objectively select rising leaders based on directly relevant skills and experience as well as skills adjacencies. And on the talent acquisition side of the house, it provides clearer role descriptions and recruitment direction so talent acquisition professionals can make more educated choices regarding candidates to fill your most critical roles.

SPOTLIGHT ON TRINET
Workforce management technology provider cut recruitment costs by deploying talent intelligence to surface quality internal talent.

TriNet is a cloud-based professional employer organization for small and medium-sized businesses. The company has approximately 16,000 customers and manages 23,000 worksite employees. It hires 400 people per year, primarily in frontline sales and customer service roles, from entry-level (individual contributor) to executive-level.

TriNet sought out talent intelligence with the primary goal of increasing candidate quality and reactivating the applicants in the company's applicant tracking system. The firm also wanted to simplify the number of point solutions used for recruiting, better enable employees to manage their careers, create a hiring tool that recruiters and hiring managers could "live in," and enable a data-driven approach to career progression and performance reviews.

To get started, the firm looked closely at the current recruitment technology stack and concluded that a number of bespoke solutions should expire. As part of an internal change management initiative, the company launched an AI-based internal hiring and training tool and had internal influencers encourage adoption.

Once the tool was in wide circulation, executives and hiring managers went from examining LinkedIn resumes one by one to viewing anonymized links to relevant internal profiles offered by the talent intelligence platform. The tool ranked internal candidates against each other according to position skill requirements and suggested who to approach first, second, and third.

TriNet realized an improvement in its average time-to-fill and time-to-submit ratio and also saw increases in the number of internal versus external hires. Application volumes jumped, particularly for re-activated candidates, and TriNet could now filter for qualified but unorthodox candidates and surface this intelligence to leadership. The company saved more than $2 million by cutting down on the use of staffing agencies and automated sourcing tools.

TriNet also used talent intelligence to initiate benchmarking on diversity metrics. The organization implemented a DEI dashboard that provided leaders with instant visibility into where candidates are coming from, how well minority groups are represented internally, and where gaps exist relative to the larger market.

How talent intelligence uses data and aggregate learning

We've talked a lot so far about what talent intelligence accomplishes, and in the last section, we explained how it helps you assess the skills of your workforce. But we're missing one major component, and that's the data; specifically, the input data talent intelligence acts upon and the output data it calculates.

To begin that exploration, we can look at data: specifically, what is the input data talent intelligence acts upon, and what is the output it calculates?

Talent intelligence input data examines career information about an individual that is collected from multiple internal (confidential) and external (public) sources. Generally, you can think of this input data as the information that appears on a resume: a person's jobs, titles, employers, education, and so on. The input data also includes the context around this information, such as a person's skills and the reputation of their employers and schools.

The output data is the job a person is likely to have next, including the company with which they'll work and the title they'll have. In other words, talent intelligence calculates what's next for any given person based on the model's understanding of their career information and internal and external data on available roles.

Keep in mind that a prediction is not a rule but a probability. Every person has many possible next steps in their career, each of which has a certain probability associated with it.

Here's an example of what this might look like. Let's say Jason went to college, took a job, got a master's degree, then took another job. For each step, we have information including Jason's skills and what our talent intelligence platform predicts as Jason's next career moves.

The platform also knows what jobs are available within the context of this calculation and can apply its prediction according to these available roles. And not only can it take a person and show them the best-fit jobs from a list of available positions based on what's next for them, but it can also take a job and show employers the best-fit candidates from a list of people.

Of course, a talent intelligence platform is only as strong as its ability to train itself on large volumes of data. This is called aggregate learning. The ability to aggregate data is important because a smaller volume of data from fewer sources will not be able to give the strongest predictions.

There are several reasons why a talent intelligence platform might not use aggregate learning. It might lack the technical sophistication to combine data from many sources and to build the calculations needed. Some platforms just examine your data, so the models it provides are different for every company. As you can imagine, there are drawbacks to this.

First, you'll notice that over the course of this book, we talk about bias a lot. A model built from one set of data is more likely to have bias concerns because a smaller set of data is ultimately limited.

Second, a model built from less data has fewer situations to analyze and will therefore be less accurate and more variable.

Third, you are likely to experience delays in deploying your talent intelligence system while the provider custom-creates a model from your data. You could spend months waiting for your strategy to pay dividends.

When a talent intelligence platform uses aggregate learning, all sources of data are fed into one model. Aggregate learning meets privacy and security standards, and combining data sources in this way does not expose one person's data to anyone else.

A talent intelligence platform built with aggregate learning has other advantages too. For one, the model providing predictions isn't biased against a situation it hasn't seen before. To better explain what this means, imagine you receive a job application from someone at a company you've never heard of. If no one from that company has applied to your company before, you might be biased against the candidate because you don't know anything about their current company. But a talent intelligence platform with aggregate learning has analyzed a billion careers and has definitely come across this company.

From here on out, when we refer to talent intelligence, we will assume the type that leverages aggregate learning.

Profile enrichment

A talent intelligence platform can give us more information about a candidate than a static resume or application because of profile enrichment. As we've mentioned, talent intelligence can automatically add detail to every talent profile, including in these five areas:

- **Relevance:** A talent intelligence platform highlights how much relevant experience a person has for a position. Someone may have a lot of experience, but not all of it may be important to the job you are trying to fill. The platform calculates how much of the total experience is relevant, which helps to inform an interview or hiring decision.

- **Context and timeliness:** The platform shows information about a candidate's prior experiences, most significantly the relative success your company has in hiring from a company that person worked for or a school they attended at a certain time. For instance, you can look at your dashboard and see a list of candidates who were hired from Accenture in the early '00s.

- **Career highlights:** A talent intelligence platform notes if a candidate has special career experience relative to their peers. For example, it would call out if an individual reached a mid-level management position faster than others in that role.

- **Similarity:** Sometimes, your first-choice candidate will go somewhere else. This type of platform shows you a list of other candidates who closely resemble the first choice. In the same way, it can also show a candidate a list of similar jobs.

- **Skills:** Talent intelligence understands the skills the candidate actually has, not just the skills they claim to have. The platform calculates this information from existing profile content and prior jobs and education. It also compares the person's provable skills against the skills needed for the job and shows you the gap. Talent intelligence also allows us to look at skill patterns, such as the age or recency of a skill in people in a given network.

This last bullet, "skills," deserves a closer look. Talent intelligence platforms understand that candidates with similar professional backgrounds likely have similar skills. For example, the platform can infer the skills of an individual who lists only their job titles and prior companies, based on the explicit skills of individuals who have the same career experience and provide substantial detail of their work. The platform can also understand the skills required for a job based on the tens of millions of job descriptions that it has interpreted from across the globe in every industry.

Many advanced skills require other, more basic skills. Candidates who list those higher-level capabilities are almost certain to have mastered lower-level skills. A teacher, for example, might say in their biography that they won an award, or improved student test scores. They might omit that they spent years taking complicated subjects and explaining them simply. Or, they might omit that they know how to capture the attention of dozens of people who are easily distracted. Talent intelligence makes these inferences from a massive number of candidate profiles and job descriptions. It provides additional skills analysis in four ways:

- **Validated skills:** These are skills that the individual has claimed to have and the platform can confirm the individual has these skills with a high degree of likelihood.

- **Likely skills:** These are skills that the individual is highly likely to have, but that the individual has not specifically claimed. The talent intelligence platform may show likely skills for a role if the individual has listed a job title and company but no further information. An interviewer can ask a candidate about these skills.

- **Skills to validate:** These are skills that are listed as necessary for a position and are claimed by the individual, but the platform cannot confirm that the individual has these skills based on the skills of individuals with similar profiles.

- **Missing skills:** These are skills that are listed as necessary for a position but the individual does not claim these skills and the platform cannot confirm that the individual has these skills based on the skills of individuals with similar profiles. Again, an interviewer may wish to ask the individual about these.

Data normalization

When you have a lot of data, you'll have variations—meaning the same thing will be expressed in different ways and different concepts may use the same text.

Humans can understand variation from context, but artificial intelligence may not. We once coped with this through master data management, which combined human analysts and digital tools to manually clean up data.

Now, however, there's data normalization. A talent intelligence platform understands nuances in the data and presents them accurately to you the first time. To clarify this point, here are a few examples:

- **Keyword matching:** The abbreviation "St" can mean Street or Saint, and talent intelligence will understand which is which.
- **Names:** Talent intelligence creates a single talent record for an individual. It's common for a company to have multiple versions of a person's profile, generally one for each time they applied for a job. Imagine that Joe Smith applied for a job three times in a decade, each time with a different resume. A talent intelligence platform will recognize that it's the same Joe Smith, combine the three records, remove duplicate entries, and show a single profile for Joe Smith. It also won't confuse this Joe Smith with another Joe Smith who has also applied.
- **Titles:** Talent intelligence knows whether a "doctor" is a medical doctor or a person with a PhD in another field.

- **Addresses:** Addresses can be presented in a variety of ways, especially if candidates reside in different countries. Talent intelligence platforms recognize addresses even if building numbers, for instance, appear after the street name as opposed to before.

Let's also call out that this type of context matching works in languages besides English, including those with gendered nouns and other language trickeries!

SPOTLIGHT ON AUTOMATION ANYWHERE
RPA provider adopted talent intelligence to match existing candidate records with newly calibrated open roles.

Automation Anywhere is a global leader in robotic process automation, empowering software bots—or digital workers that perform repetitive or manual tasks—to improve customer productivity and engagement.

Automation Anywhere has 1,600 employees and a few hundred open positions at any given time, most of which are in sales and engineering. The company has 15 global offices and distributed professionals spread across the world.

Automation Anywhere's applicant tracking system contains nearly 200,000 candidate records, but there has been no good way to search them. So, if a person applied to a job and was not hired, they were rarely considered for a later role even if their skills were a match for a different or new role. Over time, the candidate records grew stale because the resumes were never updated after the initial application.

Director of recruiting operations Ashlee Duran-Booshehri manages a team of coordinators and program managers and executes background checks, offer letters, scheduling, referrals, reporting and analytics, and immigration to-dos. As the company grew, so did the challenges of finding the right candidates and then moving them through the hiring process efficiently.

Automation Anywhere adopted a talent intelligence platform to crack open the treasure trove of its applicant tracking system. After starting with role calibration, a process in which recruiters and hiring managers work together to outline a set of job competencies, the company would consult the platform for a top recommendation within the 200,000-strong network. The suggested candidate could be a past applicant, an employee referral, or even a former employee. Using publicly available data, the platform has automatically updated this candidate's profile since the last time they engaged with the company!

"We used to have one person apply for one job and that was it," said Duran-Booshehri. "Now an applicant can potentially be a match for all kinds of jobs."

When you only have an applicant tracking system, it's difficult to see all the interactions the company has had with a candidate, provided those connection points involved multiple managers for multiple roles. When you layer talent intelligence onto an applicant tracking system, Duran-Booshehri told us: "You can see all the job requisitions one candidate spans. This viewpoint has brought candidates to the forefront we never would have looked at before."

Automation Anywhere also filters its list of prospects to boost diversity. The talent intelligence platform ensures recruiters aren't ruling out women for sales roles, for instance, and recalibrates job descriptions to expand a pool if necessary.

The company also uses the platform to find the right prospects by role, region, or diversity—and then sends out targeted messages, letting them know what the company is up to and telling them, "Hey, we'd love to have you be a part of this."

Using talent intelligence, Automation Anywhere filled as many roles in a quarter as it did during the entire previous year. The human talent acquisition team has been 3.5 times more productive, and time to fill has decreased approximately 30 percent from 65 to 45 days.

The interview process is far more time efficient too. "Because applicants are more likely to already be a part of the company's network, they are familiar with us," said Duran-Booshehri.

"They've often already been vouched for and can skip a recruiter screen." Multiply that saved half an hour by thousands of candidates, and it's easy to see how Automation Anywhere's human recruiters do so much more without needing to staff up.

Can talent intelligence be multi-platform?

Organizations have invested in a variety of solutions to address specific facets of the talent journey, including applicant tracking systems, onboarding portals, and learning management systems. As a result, they have acquired significant amounts of information which, when consolidated and consumed by talent intelligence, can deliver outsized value to internal and external stakeholders.

While using point solutions can produce talent intelligence, we believe there are significant advantages to using a single platform, namely, the interconnectedness of talent acquisition and management, the need for strategic planning and execution across the talent spectrum, and the ability to unlock the rich talent data typically fragmented across different systems and tools.

The foundation of the talent management technology stack is typically a human resources management system (HRMS) that performs core HR functions such as payroll and benefits plan administration. This stack is commonly bolstered with other standalone solutions for managing candidates, moving people internally, measuring productivity, performing career and succession planning, and upskilling existing employees.

As companies increasingly look to their own organizations as a source of talent, compelling synergies between talent acquisition and management systems are gaining attention. As we've already discussed, any organization looking to hire should first consider whether it already has the talent to meet that need. Even an organization staffing a short-term project might find they have the right skills available inside.

As another example, candidate engagement technology can easily be used with internal employees: why pay for two systems that provide essentially the same service to two audiences? Furthermore, every employee retained is one less candidate that needs to be recruited. So, creating an employee experience that encourages people to stay and fends off recruitment efforts by competitors is actually an important component of a talent acquisition strategy.

Also, whether they are currently a candidate or an employee, people typically view their career as a single journey. Implementing a system that supports the needs of the individual throughout their career aligns better with what your people want.

Single platforms encourage a holistic talent strategy

Properly supporting individual employee journeys requires a holistic talent strategy. As we've briefly touched on, forming such a strategy starts with gaining a solid understanding of internal capabilities against current and future needs. This boils down to determining what talent your organization needs today, what talent you currently have, and identifying and correcting the short-term and long-term gaps between those two states.

This investigative process assesses how your full-time and contingent talent is currently used, where that talent may be best deployed in the future, and whether you can get where you need to go via short-term project staffing or tying into a candidate or employee's long-term career trajectory. It's essentially a macro analysis of hiring needs based on your business's unique requirements and demands. It describes the end state your organization wishes to achieve. However, it doesn't yet prescribe how to get there.

Analyzing internal capabilities manifests as an internal organization-wide talent graph. Technology that supports this should, at a minimum, be able to facilitate internal talent profiles, including current job responsibilities and skills not leveraged in an employee's current role.

A secondary component of internal capabilities is employee potential and mapping. Organizations can use a single talent intelligence platform to track employees' career goals and progressions, determine what they are capable of, and enable them to better plan their careers. Single platforms facilitate internal gig work, meaning they assist employees in identifying opportunities they may never have found outside their current functional area.

Combined with strategic and succession planning, talent intelligence identifies skills areas that are currently weak and recommends the best course of action for staffing those skills. A single-platform solution is more likely to tap into a variety of HR-related data and recommend uncommon career paths that a human recruiter or hiring manager might otherwise miss.

Finally, when talent intelligence is integrated into a single platform, organizations can understand the real-time dynamics between skill requirements, internal training, and external hiring—at scale. Siloed data is one of the biggest challenges facing companies trying their hands at AI, and a unified talent platform allows us to unearth insights across the spectrum of talent acquisition and employee experience.

In short, using one solution rather than many allows for more efficient execution of a holistic and integrated talent strategy.

Hopefully, you now have a more concrete understanding of how talent intelligence works, namely that it dynamically self-learns to master the available skills and potential of a company's existing workforce and the larger market. In the next chapter, we'll delve into exactly how talent intelligence can facilitate skill acquisition and the movement of talent from one type of role to another.

APPLY THE AI

Your company, FutureStrong, has too many point solutions, with separate providers for talent acquisition, benefits administration, onboarding, learning, and performance management. The oldest and clunkiest of these solutions is FutureStrong's recruitment portal. The company's time to fill keeps lengthening and it is continually losing new hires at the preboarding stage.

You would like to see these systems substantially more integrated and infused with artificial intelligence, but it will take some upfront investment. In the space below, write the beginning of a business case for your CEO for why a single-platform talent intelligence solution may be the best course of action.

Chapter summary

- If you haven't yet outlined your **professional capabilities** and don't have **capability leaders** governing your functional areas, you might want to think about your **job architecture** redesign from a fresh perspective.

- **Talent intelligence** platforms examine skill adjacency and context to determine current organizational capabilities and future needs. They also provide a consistent and unbiased evaluation of individual capabilities against globally standardized job descriptions and requirements.

- To explore how talent intelligence works, we can look at data; specifically, the input data talent intelligence acts upon and the output data it calculates.

- A talent intelligence platform is only as strong as its ability to train itself on large volumes of data. This is called **aggregate learning**. The ability to aggregate data is important because a smaller volume of data from fewer sources will not be able to give the strongest predictions.

- A talent intelligence platform can give us more information about a candidate than a static resume or application because of profile enrichment. It can **enrich talent profiles** in the areas of relevance, context, career highlights, similarity, and skills.

- Using a **single platform solution** for talent intelligence rather than many allows for more efficient execution of a holistic and integrated talent strategy.

4

Skill acquisition and the rise of customized learning

Skill acquisition is not just a passion of Kamal's, it's an integral part of his life story. After graduating from IIT (the Indian Institutes of Technology) as an engineer and writing networking protocols for a while, Kamal realized that building a great product wasn't good enough. That product also had to be commercially successful, and you learned what would make it successful by engaging with customers. That's how Kamal found himself exploring (and loving) the worlds of marketing and business development.

Those years as a marketer and then the CMO led Kamal to sales and revenue operations and he pivoted into a new career as chief revenue officer. By again building on the foundation of his existing skills, Kamal discovered the next logical step, and eventually his experience in revenue operations led to his promotion to president of Eightfold.

Kamal's journey has so far spanned multiple industries, companies, and what has felt like lifespans. As he tried various functions, his skills increased in breadth and depth, evolving from knowledge of the product to knowledge of the market and finally to knowledge of customers and other key stakeholders. If Kamal had started in sales—without his engineering experience—he wouldn't have properly understood how a product was built and there might have been a limit to how far he could go.

This is an ideal illustration of the sometimes windy road that lies ahead for capable and ambitious professionals. Kamal himself has been inspired by what prompts people to break old habits and try new things, especially because in the decades preceding the Covid-19 pandemic, there was a global trend toward multiple careers and multiple jobs.

At the same time, the pre-pandemic period saw organizationally driven learning become less piecemeal and more cohesive, including planned upskilling and reskilling initiatives. Upskilling refers to teaching an employee to do the job they currently have better or more efficiently, and reskilling refers to training an employee to do a completely new job (we will talk more about the differences between these two strategies later in the chapter). As technology deployed learning-as-a-service, skill acquisition became more self-driven and encouraged careerists like Kamal to forge non-linear career paths.

Given that work itself is evolving to more distributed environments and fluid roles, these shifts will only continue in the coming years. This chapter will explore how and why HR leaders are using AI to build more resilient and dynamically skilled workforces during what we now see as an "age of disruption."

We'll discuss the driving forces behind improving employee skill sets, how to think about skills differently in this new climate, why a multi-pronged approach to skill acquisition works best, and last but not least, what tech-enabled skill acquisition brings to the table that traditional learning strategies can't.

Driving forces behind skillbuilding

As we talked about in Chapter 1, an ever-widening talent gap is one of the biggest issues driving the need to increase the skills of current employees. "A big challenge for us is finding enough people that are capable to do the work," said Dan Peterson, vice president for industry and government affairs at Cook Medical, of his company's struggles to fill medical device manufacturing jobs.

Peterson's company isn't alone. In addition to the 2021 Deloitte *Human Capital Trends* report we discussed earlier, we reviewed some compelling McKinsey research indicating that 87 percent of executives and managers report that they are either actively experiencing talent gaps or expect to be experiencing them soon. While most of those who responded to the McKinsey survey reported focusing on hiring to close those gaps, about a third said they had started training their employees to either perform more duties in their current roles or move into different, sometimes multiple, roles (McKinsey, 2021).

While the "Great Resignation" and pandemic-fueled remote work are certainly crucial factors, we sometimes forget that digital transformation is a major driver of skills gaps too. Alexandra is fond of talking about the need for applied technology skills—or knowing how to use available technology to do your job more efficiently. As an example, if you are a marketing executive, you probably don't need to know how to program a custom media tracking application from scratch. But you *do* need to know that technology exists to create an application that will meet your internal reporting needs.

Another dimension of applied technology skills involves the oversight of smart machines. Alexandra likes to say that wherever a piece of automation or algorithm is inserted into a traditionally human-driven process, you need a person to build it, manage it, understand its output, fix it when it breaks, and explain what it does to decision-makers. Considering machine participation is everywhere, humans who have the skills to collaborate with them are essential. Therefore, regardless of your industry, title, or function, the development of applied technology skills is necessary.

The financial constraints imposed by the Covid-19 pandemic are also prompting increased internal skill acquisition. A need for frugality has hiring managers focusing more on upskilling and reskilling current employees than hiring new ones. "It's more cost-efficient and far more effective to build critical skills from within," wrote Josh Bersin. According to his research, it can cost six times more to hire externally than to build new skills internally (Bersin, 2019).

As reported by the Society for Human Resource Management, this cost differential goes a long way in explaining why nearly 70 percent of organizations sustained their employee training budgets despite the chaos of the pandemic. "Despite these unpredictable times, many employers are maintaining their upskilling and reskilling initiatives, which is critical to maximizing talent and bridging the skills gap," said Trent Burner, vice president of SHRM Research (Gurchiek, 2020).

Not everyone is on the skill acquisition bandwagon, however; according to Siddhartha Gupta, CEO of Mercer Mettl, the issues that keep businesses from investing in reskilling and upskilling programs include identifying relevant skills gaps, finding the time for employee training, and budgeting correctly for the right L&D programs (Gupta, 2020).

Indeed, we've recently heard that because learning opportunities are so much more accessible today, employers want their people to bear greater responsibility for finding and taking advantage of them. However, there is a long history of organizations directing individual education that isn't so easy to forget.

Huggy Rao, whom you might recall from Chapter 2 is a professor of organizational behavior and human resources at the Stanford University School of Business, discussed this issue at the Cultivate conference in 2022. "A gentleman called Chester Bernard, who was the president of AT&T, and wrote a brilliant book in 1938 titled *The Functions of the Executive*, argued that leaders are inherently teachers and business is fundamentally an educational institution. We have a long history of corporations being sources of learning." He told our conference audience. "It's the organization's responsibility to think about the competencies employees most urgently need. On one side, there's intellectual property, which is a source of competitive advantage. And on the other, there are the skills that promote personal growth, activism, and change, which groups like the millennials value more highly."

The employer must offer opportunities for both while respecting the individual's freedom to choose the learning method that's best for them.

Are we doing corporate learning right?

When Rao thinks about the elements of corporate learning that organizations need to hone, he considers two factors: curiosity and generosity. "Many of today's employees don't think of a lengthy career horizon. They think of a tour of duty, three to four years tops. So, what are the skills we can give them now along the curiosity and generosity dimensions?" he said.

As to whether we're collectively doing a good job with this, Rao has mixed feelings. "I hear a lot of rhetoric about people being human assets, but I see corporations doing little. Corporations give people limited, non-specific training while they're there. But knowing what employees want, why can't we create a portable learning budget? You put money into an employee's account and the employee decides what is best for them. If they are asked to leave the company, the two-to-three-year learning budget travels with them to further augment their skills."

Rao believes talent acquisition should focus on the approach of: "If you join our company, we promise that you will grow." And this means we can't be homogeneous with our learning options.

Now certain industries operate with very thin margins, and it's difficult to justify a lot of education investment. The retail sector is an example of this—employees come in and out and investment in people tends to be "spray and pray," like a broad-spectrum antibiotic rather than a more targeted solution like gene therapy. And this approach certainly doesn't help with the retail industry's characteristically high turnover rates.

When they do invest, many organizations tend to focus training efforts in the wrong direction. Rao told us about a John Deere study that examined the skills of the most successful internal salespeople. To his surprise, the best salespeople weren't the ones trained extensively on product knowledge, but the ones who had mastered the art of nonverbal communication. When they were face to face with a prospect, they responded in a way that mirrored the potential client and in doing so, established trust. So, in this company with this group of salespeople, it was more useful to increase nonverbal communication skills than product knowledge.

This wasn't a surprise to us. Many organizations could improve the ways in which they educate employees for career durability, or the ability to sustain gainful employment over an extended period in various functions. Career durability has five components, and not only is it exactly what most employees are looking for and need in their careers, it's also what ultimately makes them more versatile for the organization. Some of these probably sound familiar, including the applied technology skills we mentioned earlier:

- **Soft skills** are interpersonal attributes that you need to collaborate **successfully** with others at work. As machines take over more work tasks over the next 10 years, soft skills like empathy, intuition, diplomacy, judgment, and problem solving will set human employees apart.

- **Hard skills** are those in a specific area for which learning can be measured (i.e. you either know it or you don't).

- **Applied technology skills** represent the ability to leverage people, processes, data, and devices to do a job more efficiently.

- **Institutional knowledge** is industry-specific expertise gained through experience and/or tenure. Some things can only be learned by facing similar scenarios multiple times over a career lifespan.

- **A growth mindset** is the positive attitude that influences how an individual sees their world, and that motivates them to learn and change.

Career durability is essential for everyone, but how it shows up, and what is needed to build it, is highly specific to the individual. Like all learning initiatives, those developed to address career durability must be significantly personalized.

We admit that it isn't easy for companies to surmount the issues associated with rolling out individualized learning programs. But with the right plan in place, a company of any size can customize reskilling and upskilling opportunities. Understanding the reasons for upskilling and reskilling and then committing to an investment are critical steps, but choosing and implementing a methodology is a taller order. Let's use the next several pages to talk about the building blocks of an AI-infused learning strategy.

SPOTLIGHT ON EY SKILLS FOUNDRY

HR consulting giant built an upskilling program based on live "supply and demand" data.

In recent years, EY witnessed its main clientele expanding beyond the CHRO to include chief operating officers, chief financial officers, and line of business leaders who were actively addressing HR-related challenges such as return to work, productivity, and employee well-being. The team was hearing the same refrains over and over: despite an insatiable demand for upskilling and reskilling, organizations were not prepared and lacked skills, capabilities, and learning scale.

To solve this problem, EY focused brainstorming efforts on a "humans at the center" approach and the freedom to reimagine its own—and clients'—workforce agendas. A key insight was revealed through this iterative process: despite being in the learning business for decades, EY itself wasn't doing enough to keep its top talent learning, engaged, and committed to the organization. As people advisory service leader Mike Bertolino explained during the recent Cultivate conference, the team saw that offering alternate career paths to ambitious employees was no longer optional.

EY responded by building its own upskilling program called the EY Skills Foundry. Now used internally and with clients, the Skills Foundry encompasses a live heat map of skills across the organization, showing both supply and demand and allowing for faster decision making around upskilling and reskilling investments. It also includes AI-driven components that speed and scale training, and a validated and secure digital record of employees' skills and experiences.

The EY team tested the Skills Foundry platform extensively, applying automation when possible and seeking input and refinements from clients. EY encourages customers to use the Foundry by pointing to its own internal success with its 300,000-strong workforce. As customer zero for this offering, EY has shown customers exactly how they can make a difference by tracking skills and matching talented people to desirable opportunities. And by developing a series of learning academies that cover a range of topics, EY is an instrumental part of an expansive global effort to define and teach the skills its AI-powered platform suggests will be most valuable in the near future.

Thinking about jobs differently

Recent news stories have focused on the challenges of filling unskilled and low-skilled positions. Difficulty hiring for positions traditionally seen as unskilled, like restaurant service, has prompted some businesses and legislators to claim that an unsolvable labor shortage exists.

As a rule, a shortage of people or skills is not the problem. Rather, as we've mentioned, the challenge lies in reconsidering how to measure and match workers' skills to organizational needs. So, the first step in creating an effective learning strategy is to reconsider how you think about jobs and skills.

As we addressed in the last chapter, a cornerstone of talent intelligence is identifying skills areas that are currently weak and recommending the best course of action for staffing those skills. In the context of learning, this involves conceptualizing workers as people who build and use skills throughout their daily lives. To fully benefit from a skills-based approach, companies need to think of their own teams as consisting of skill sets rather than discrete roles.

Granted, this concept is not easy to understand or implement because we are accustomed to thinking of a single job and a single skill as interrelated. Here's one way to go about it. You can begin by reassessing the skills used daily by your existing team. For example, the pandemic pushed many workers to acquire a new set of applied technology skills related to communication, like videoconferencing aplomb and online team collaboration. For many employers, these rapid changes also mean existing job descriptions are outdated.

Next, consider which of the skills needed for each job are technical, job-specific skills, and which are transferable skills that may be learned in a variety of contexts. You can deploy talent intelligence to understand the transferable skills each of your roles can use and whether a candidate previously had a related job or not. This broader view allows HR teams and hiring managers to look beyond former job titles to the capabilities developed throughout a worker's lifespan.

Another way to cultivate a skills-based view is to step outside demands for degrees or certifications. "Employers looking to build or rebuild the skill base of their workforces will find they have more options if they look beyond traditional education credentials and experience requirements," wrote Michael Burt and Bryan Gormley of the Conference Board of Canada (Burt and Gormley, 2021).

Hiring teams that require certain college degrees or credentials for certain jobs automatically exclude qualified candidates from consideration. "Instead of screening out by pedigree, smart employers are increasingly screening in talent for performance and potential," said Byron Auguste, co-founder and CEO at Opportunity@Work (Vander Ark, 2021).

By focusing on workers' capabilities, companies can build a broader pool of diverse, qualified candidates. These smart employers avail themselves of the skills and abilities candidates have learned during the pandemic, for instance, even if those same candidates' traditional path toward a college degree or promotion was disrupted. Think about this for a moment. Covid-19 caused rapid, widespread social upheaval and forced many people to develop new skills in communication, problem solving, flexibility, and adaptability. As skills like this support success in any role, they can be found in a wide range of available candidates, regardless of where and how the candidate learned them.

Is there a documented labor shortage in many fields? Absolutely, and we said as much in Chapter 1. But summarily blaming this shortage on a lack of worker skills misrepresents the nature of the challenge companies face. Thinking of workers in terms of their specific training for specific roles no longer serves us. Instead, companies that are building sustainable growth are doing so by thinking about skills in a broader manner.

A multi-pronged approach to skill acquisition

It's one thing to identify the individual skills you need to acquire within your workforce, but it's quite another to put real training programs in place. And in many cases, this is where organizations falter. Either learning programs are standalone and don't relate to the larger organizational strategy, or they are presented as one-size-fits-all endeavors that inevitably miss the target with some of their audience.

We'll devote most of this section to creating effective training programs, but first, let's go into a bit more detail about the type of skill acquisition you'll need. Recall first that upskilling enhances a person's performance in their current role and prepares them to progress at their job. This approach gives employees the skills they need to take on new responsibilities within their position, like being promoted to manager in their department.

On the other hand, reskilling helps employees move permanently into new roles or adjust to significant changes in their current roles. An example would be training a receptionist to take on marketing tasks after your company adopts an AI-based phone answering system. And cross-skilling, a relatively new concept, prepares individuals with supplementary skills that allow them to temporarily shift from one role to another as organizational needs dictate. Cross-trained workers can fill in at other positions within their departments, such as an event planner who takes over the duties of a social media marketing manager.

Leaders often ask us whether they should focus initially on upskilling or reskilling/cross-skilling, and you can probably guess our answer. All three have their place in today's business environment. "When it comes to rapid employee development, most companies are focusing on a hybrid approach of reskilling and upskilling, and are adopting cross-functional training programs to keep employee skill sets relevant to their organizational requirements," agreed Vinay Ravindran, a senior HR manager at SG Analytics (Ravindran, 2021).

Regardless of your intent to upskill, reskill, or cross-skill, developing effective training programs for your employees takes forethought and planning. You can't just pick a training program online, stick your employees in front of a laptop to hear a presentation, and then send them back to work expecting them to retain or use anything they may have learned. To use learning-oriented AI to the best of its potential, you must first establish a learning culture and put your humans in the best possible position to acquire new skills.

This means creating a culture where everyone understands that learning isn't a one-time event or presentation but rather an ongoing process. It's about creating a desire to learn and improve. When everyone genuinely embraces this, upskilling, reskilling, and cross-skilling programs are more effective overall. To encourage your employees to develop skills, trigger their curiosity by showing them what they don't know and rewarding them for taking the steps to investigate new ideas further.

Training programs should always help the individual as well as the company. Not everyone needs the same set of skills or the same type of training because after all we all have our individual backgrounds, roles, and plans. Leaders should tap employee aspirations and create highly personalized training programs that people will be motivated to complete, as opposed to group training that's beneficial for some and a waste of time for others.

One hallmark of the personalized program is its delivery method. Some people learn better through webinars, while others prefer live instruction and hands-on opportunities. Some employees like to master new material in short bursts, while others appreciate a lengthier approach. Ask your employees about the methods that would make them most likely to consume the information.

With all the talk of AI in this book, it's tempting to forget the person-to-person contact that has been essential to skill acquisition since apprenticeships in the Middle Ages. Now that learning programs are more customized than ever, it's even more critical for managers or mentors (or both) to keep tabs on employees during the skillbuilding process.

Traditionally, mentorship programs have varied from conversationally informal to rigidly scripted in terms of what a pair is expected to accomplish. In this context, we recommend implementing a mentorship program that specifically helps employees integrate new skills into their daily work lives. Mentors who have mastered these new skills already and are therefore able to offer insider knowledge of how new knowledge can be assimilated are ideal choices. They don't necessarily have to be senior to the employee either. The learning mix that is upskilling, reskilling, and cross-skilling favors a variety of pairings, including people who are the same level. It all depends on what the individual needs to learn and the partner who is best equipped to help in that circumstance.

Self-service is another essential element of strong skill acquisition. This phrase is well worn, but it has mainly been confined to automating tasks and handing those tasks to employees, not putting them in the driver's seat of their careers. Now, however, some organizations are offering their employees "career hubs" or portals where they can find and sign up for training and mentors based on their goals and interests.

When the millennials were starting off in the business world, they ushered in an era of experiential learning. So now that they're a majority of the workforce, it makes sense that nearly all modern skill acquisition initiatives have an on-the-job component. Today's internal talent marketplaces enable employees to identify in-house projects they can take on based on their existing skills. If the employee who wants the internal gig is missing a skill, we now have the means to direct them to the proper training, which leads us right into the next section!

Customizing individualized career plans sounds sensible, but when you have 100 or even tens of thousands of employees, it becomes difficult to do without the help of talent intelligence. Using talent intelligence baked into your existing learning management system, you can serve up reskilling, upskilling, and cross-skilling opportunities across courses, mentors, and projects based on current skills and career aspirations. By inviting every individual to develop their skills and engaging each employee at their pace, you'll facilitate a culture of personalized, continuous learning.

SPOTLIGHT ON VODAFONE
Multinational telecommunications company is building an AI-based platform integrating skills assessment with career and succession planning.

As of this book's writing, Vodafone, a British multinational telecommunications company, is creating an AI-based learning experience platform to support its strategy of becoming a market-leading technology communications company.

The platform will manage staff resourcing, skills assessment, and learning and development activities and has already been rolled out to 96,000 employees in 43 countries. It has replaced Vodafone's disparate and heavily localized HR systems, streamlining processes and aggregating data in the process.

"Our strategy as an organization is to become a technology communications company, which means we're looking to hire about 7,000 software engineers to support our aims," said Marc Starfield, Vodafone's group head of HR. "But in wanting to attract the biggest and brightest minds, we need to offer them a rich digital experience and also have an effective means of upgrading our talent in the future."

Next up for Vodafone's learning experience platform is an AI-based talent attraction and skills assessment module that will integrate with other

HR processes, such as career and succession planning. "At its core, the system is about making learning personal and purposeful, so knowing what skills you have, where you want to go, what you'll need in three years' time, and following recommendations on the learning required to get there," said Starfield. "It allows us to bring together content from Vodafone and others, like LinkedIn, in one place, and use skills targeting to connect cohorts of people who want to develop in a certain direction, all as a single experience."

The upshot, Starfield speculated, is that within three years, cost-to-hire savings should be significant. This includes a reduction in the amount of external recruitment expenditure required, because this activity will increasingly be conducted by a global business shared services center.

Process efficiency due to automation is also expected to rise by 25 percent. The total cost of ownership of the company's HR technology stack is anticipated to drop by 10 percent, while expenditure on learning content is likewise estimated to fall.

Starfield believes it is vital to focus on the people rather than the technology side of the equation. This involves being clear about what skills are valuable to different job roles and how employees should use the system. It also includes understanding how content and nudges can best be employed to support learning, listen to employees, and measure the candidate experience with data.

A short journey into tech-enabled skill acquisition

When we talk to clients about infusing AI and talent intelligence into learning initiatives, people sometimes respond with a look of fear. Incorporating "advanced" technology like this feels overwhelming, and inevitably out of scope. We therefore thought it would be helpful to illustrate examples of organizations mastering the fundamentals of smart machine participation in learning. In many cases, moving to personalized skill acquisition hasn't involved as big a leap as one might suspect.

AT&T

Upon examination, AT&T found that only about half of its employees had the STEM skills the company would require of its workers in the future. Bill Blasé, senior executive vice president of human resources at AT&T, told us that the company had two choices. "We could go out and try to hire all these software and engineering people and probably pay through the nose to get them, but even that wouldn't have been adequate. Or we could try to reskill our existing workforce so they could be competent in the technology and the skills required to run the business going forward."

AT&T chose the latter path, building an AI-based career portal that allows employees to envision their future careers and plot out the skills they will need to learn to make those futures a reality. Where AT&T lacked content for certain employee skills, it partnered with outside educational providers to bring learning programs into the portal.

PwC

PwC's Digital Fitness app encourages employees to assess their digital knowledge and create customized learning plans. Through the app, they receive learning assets to "help our people think differently and unlock their innovative creativity at scale," said Joe Atkinson, vice chair and chief products and technology officer at PwC, in a LinkedIn article (Atkinson, 2019).

The Digital Lab promotes AI-assisted collaboration. "Digital Lab is a democratized platform, which uses social and gamification features to incentivize building and sharing of assets with wide applicability," Sarah McEneaney, digital talent leader at PwC U.S., said (BasuMallick, 2021). Through the platform, employees not only learn from one another but also apply their new skills.

Accenture

In 2021, Accenture invested nearly $1 billion to reskill its workforce (Sweet, 2021). Central to the initiative is the company's

Connected Learning Platform, which is a blend of classroom and digital learning opportunities with content from internal and external subject matter experts.

"Our people learn best by connecting, collaborating, and practicing for the scenarios they will encounter in their work with our clients," said Ellyn Shook, chief leadership and human resources officer for Accenture. "From basic skills to industry-specific content, learning is available to all our people anywhere, anytime—and, in many cases, no selection or approval is involved. Simply tap the app and start learning."

Accenture's autonomous learning approach demonstrates what this chapter is all about: namely, that organizations can harness technology to give employees control over their own learning and career development.

Amazon

In keeping with the concepts of career durability and applied technology skills, Amazon launched its Upskilling 2025 initiative to prepare workers for a digitized workplace. "We think it's important to invest in our employees, help them gain new skills, and create more options for themselves," said Beth Galetti, senior VP of people experience and technology at Amazon (Amazon, 2020).

One opportunity offered through the initiative is the Mechatronics and Robotics Apprenticeship Program. In the two-phase program, existing Amazon employees attend classes and receive on-the-job training in preparation for work as mechatronics and robotics technicians. After finishing the program, these employees are poised to secure more highly compensated employment opportunities inside or outside Amazon.

Hopefully, you now have a handle on how to think about skills in a new way and are leaving this chapter with some ideas about how to leverage technology to approach skill acquisition in fresh and innovative ways. This knowledge will come in handy as we move into the next chapter on the upskilling and reskilling of diverse worker populations.

APPLY THE AI

To date, FutureStrong's L&D function has not kept up with the various skills employees must acquire to be, well, future strong. The company currently offers product-centric training via a standard online portal. Not only is the content narrow in scope, but FutureStrong lacks data-driven insight on whether it helps employees do their jobs better.

Using what you now know about talent intelligence and the importance of career durability, what initial step might you take to customize the experience for each employee?

Chapter summary

- The issues that keep businesses from investing in reskilling and upskilling programs include **identifying relevant skills gaps, finding the time for employee training,** and **budgeting correctly** for the right L&D programs.

- Many organizations could improve the ways in which they educate employees for **career durability,** or the ability to sustain gainful employment over an extended period in various functions. Career durability is essential for everyone, but how it shows up, and what is needed to build it, is highly specific to the individual.

- To think about jobs and skills differently, begin by reassessing which skills are used daily by your existing team. Next, consider which skills needed for each job are technical, job-specific skills, and which are **transferable skills** that may be learned in a variety of contexts. You can deploy **talent intelligence** software to understand the transferable skills each of your roles can use, whether a candidate previously had a related job or not.

- It's one thing to identify the individual skills you need to acquire within your workforce, but it's quite another to put real training programs in place. And in many cases, this is where organizations falter. Either learning programs are **piecemeal and don't relate** to the larger organizational strategy, or they are presented as **one-size-fits-all endeavors** that inevitably miss the target with some of their audience.

- Regardless of your intent to upskill, reskill, or cross-skill, developing **effective training programs** for your employees takes forethought and planning. To use learning-oriented AI to the best of its potential, you must first establish a **learning culture** and put your humans in the best possible position to acquire new skills.

- **Customizing individualized career plans** may sound sensible, but when you have 100 or even tens of thousands of employees, it becomes difficult to do. Using talent intelligence, baked into your existing learning management system, you can serve up **reskilling, upskilling,** and **cross-skilling** opportunities across courses, mentors, and projects based on current skills and career aspirations.

5

Diversity is everyone's issue

There has been a lot of chatter around diversity, equity, and inclusion over the last few years, but have you noticed that the discussion is often rather superficial? Talking about this amongst ourselves, we noted that positive intent is there. Most organizations want to be more diverse, and are good at admiring the problem. But the desire to change is currently backed up with little meaningful action.

Kamal's interest in DEI issues stems from discussions around women as an under-represented workforce segment. This has never made sense to him. There's no job around today that a woman can't do. There are more women than men in the world overall, and more women than men are graduating from college. How can we say that we can't find someone who can do X when millions of qualified women are staring us in the face?

Kamal feels that if we don't do a better job of solving systemic bias against women, we can't solve it for other under-represented groups. This is why women are a great place to start when it comes to using talent intelligence to identify capabilities objectively and override the human habit of unconscious bias.

In 2030, the companies dominating your industry will be the ones investing in DEI initiatives, platforms, and strategies today. Effective DEI requires a balance between talent intelligence platforms and excellent change-management programs to make inclusion a core part of a company's culture.

Based on conversations with a group of CHROs in our network, the current approach of "we're fine because we can still collect a massive number of resumes" isn't working. Neither is the use of outdated keyword matching and decades-old applicant tracking systems. ATS (applicant tracking systems) are so broken they would have overlooked Leonardo da Vinci based on his resume alone. No one wants to pass over the next genius to redefine an industry with their inventions, insights, and patents.

The CHROs in the authors' networks define diversity as the ability to attract, nurture, recruit, and retain candidates and employees regardless of race, gender, age, educational background, culture, sexual orientation, ethnicity, or physicality. One CHRO told us that diversity initiatives in talent management must also consider the experiential aspects of each person, including their life experiences, education, relationships, previous and current job roles, and innate neural characteristics including emotion, personality, and cognitive styles.

Inclusion, on the other hand, means that candidates and employees know they are valued, and that their insights and opinions matter. Our CHRO contacts have been nearly unanimous in saying their most effective talent programs are built on a foundation of diversity, and that their organizations' efforts at inclusion are a work in progress.

Concentrating too much on diversity and not enough on inclusion can backfire and can lead to diverse candidates feeling like part of an experiment or socially driven cause, instead of being respected for their unique capacities and skills. When diverse candidates sense that the effort at inclusion is secondary, unconscious biases often emerge and conflict begins.

You may already be familiar with the many business cases for DEI, but a refresher can never hurt. Let's start with the fact that the more diverse and inclusive any organization is, the more profitable and innovative it is. McKinsey's *Delivering Through Diversity* report found that organizations in the top quartile for ethnic/cultural diversity on executive teams were 33 percent more likely to have industry-leading profitability (Hunt et al, 2018).

An American Sociological Association study uncovered that companies with the highest levels of racial diversity attain 15 times the sales revenues of those organizations with the lowest levels of diversity (ASA, 2009). And recent *Forbes* research showed that 56 percent of international business leaders feel that diversity is a catalyst for greater innovation (Forbes Insights, 2020).

These and hundreds of other studies conclusively prove that DEI delivers lasting, measurable gains to the innovative strength of any business. One example of this involves individuals with physical disabilities. The unemployment rates in this population are sky high and largely for no reason given that most office spaces are accessible and many people are working remotely. In fact, people with physical disabilities have prompted experimentation (such as text-based collaboration for hearing-impaired employees) that actually makes distributed work environments easier for everyone.

Another important factor is customers. Organizations competing in flat- and no-growth industries are struggling to reposition their most popular products to attract the fastest-growing minority groups and market segments that didn't exist when the products were created.

CHROs are tasked with finding diverse design, engineering, and service teams that reflect the perspective of their customers, and which can revitalize products that may be out of touch with customers' current and future needs.

This brings us to the next major benefit of DEI, which is decision making. Per a recent study by Cloverpop, the more diverse a team, the better decisions it makes 87 percent of the time. Decisions that were both made and executed by gender-diverse teams performed 6 percent better than average. Adding age diversity increased performance to 45 percent above average. When geographic diversity was added, decision-making performance jumped by 60 percent (Larson, 2017).

Many leadership and management theorists call this the Medici Effect. Researchers who specialize in the Medici Effect cite the exponential gains in art, astronomy, science, and engineering in Florence, Italy during the 15th century, when several different cultures started working together. When an organizational culture emphasizes inclusion, "groupthink" is challenged, dissenting views are encouraged, and profits grow.

Organizations and the CHROs leading them are measuring DEI progress beyond profits, however. We've talked with several who are intensely focused on how the less easily quantifiable aspects of a successful DEI strategy are redefining the very nature of their businesses.

According to our CHRO network, effective CEO collaboration can make or break a DEI strategy. Subordinates look to leaders' behaviors for cues as to what is and isn't acceptable. CHROs say that when C-level peers and their direct reports choose to model a more open, inclusive way of communicating and operating their business units, they achieve the greatest results.

We have learned that lip service doesn't work. Changing organization-wide behaviors and achieving diversity goals starts with C-level executives who are emotionally committed to DEI. Divisions, departments, and teams will only change if they see C-level executives buying completely into the direction DEI needs to survive and thrive.

"I think of inclusion as a competency. Inclusive leaders aren't necessarily born, they can be made," Jolen Anderson of BNY Mellon told us at our Cultivate conference. "This boils down to creating a sense of psychological safety across your team and bringing people with different points of view into a conversation."

Practically speaking, building the inclusion competency usually includes creating a series of planning sessions for each C-level executive with their direct reports and teams. These sessions define practical ways stronger DEI can be achieved via a more inclusive corporate environment. One CHRO confided that it took a year for their financial services company to translate the insights gained from the planning sessions into outcomes and actionable goals. The effort was worth it: today, this company has made DEI a core part of its DNA and has a single-digit attrition rate across all diversity-based hires.

A final argument for DEI involves the question of automation and human skill acquisition. As we've been talking about for a while now, within the next decade or so, a lot of human jobs with mainly physical and manual labor are likely to disappear. Carla Arellano is a partner in McKinsey's Organizational Solutions group, which supports culture through data and analytics. At the Cultivate conference in 2022, Arellano described these manual labor jobs as being part of the "fifth wage quintile." They are disproportionately held by more vulnerable populations such as immigrants, younger workers, people without college degrees, African Americans, and Latinos.

"These folks have less access to education and other advancement resources," Arellano said:

> And the problem is that when the jobs go away, many of these low-wage workers will need to move up into the higher quintiles, which require different skill levels. They don't just need to learn new skills, but also need to change how they approach finding jobs in this new territory. The steepness of the curve to reskill into these new areas is daunting.

It's undoubtedly difficult for a single individual or even a group of individuals to make this transition, but organizations can help by deploying AI-driven DEI strategies. In the remainder of this chapter, we'll explore how to build a technology-based DEI strategy in your organization, showcasing a few ways AI is helping organizations achieve their recruitment and retention objectives with racial minorities and veterans.

Technology-driven DEI strategies

Throughout this book, we've been talking about the benefits of a single platform for various areas of talent intelligence, and DEI is no exception. Closed, siloed systems lead to closed, limited thinking that limits an organization's potential to attain its DEI objectives. Without the right platform, DEI strategies can take on an optional, non-central role in any organization's current and future direction. Here's what we recommend instead:

Define, implement, and drive DEI-based recruitment strategies on a single platform

The CHROs in our network have told us they need a customizable, scalable way to target diverse candidates. As you build out a recruiting strategy, creating candidate lists without reference to factors like age, gender, ethnicity, veteran status, and disability status is one must. Getting beyond hiring quotas by having a talent intelligence platform that relies on capability matching first, without regard to any potential biasing factors, is another. Generating candidate lists based solely on skills can also help with hiring compliance requirements in specific regions and nations.

Create a candidate-focused career site

Most candidate experiences, from the very first moment, harm under-represented groups. Job descriptions often use biased language that can especially discourage women and older candidates. Organizations can fix this problem by reconfiguring their career sites to focus on candidate needs first. If every candidate is encouraged to apply for the job that best suits their potential, that experience will overcome much of the self-selection bias we see.

When your candidate comes to the career site, they should see information personalized for them. The most important question any career site visitor has is: what jobs are available for *me*? In a candidate-focused career site, your available jobs are ranked for the individual candidate and they can see exactly why they are a match (in other words, their skills and experiences that make the job a compelling option for them, and the reasons why they are a strong candidate for your organization). The act of showing a candidate how they are a great fit for a job reduces self-selection bias because candidates have varying degrees of risk tolerance, and encouragement reduces the sense of risk.

This seems obvious, but your career site's application process should be as fast and easy as possible. If it isn't, you may unknowingly eliminate busy parents and older workers from consideration. Understand that if you insist that candidates prove their interest by filling out long forms, providing unique cover letters and question answers, and taking assessment tests, your selection process is inherently biased against those who don't have the time or ability to do these things.

Prevent bias during the candidate screening and interview phases

The hiring process is naturally prone to bias. Recruiters and hiring managers see a candidate's personal characteristics, such as their perceived gender, ethnicity, age, and educational credentials, and make selection decisions based on these factors rather than on each person's potential to succeed. The result is reduced diversity.

No one does this on purpose. These biases are almost always unintentional. It's just hard for all of us, as human beings, to separate out all the factors that go into our decision making, even if we know intellectually that some factors shouldn't matter.

So once candidates are in front of hiring managers, organizations need to do everything possible to prevent bias in candidate selection. At the initial stages, the best strategy is candidate masking. Candidate masking involves blocking unconscious bias by removing all potential pieces of bias—including ethnicity and gender—from resumes so only objective data points remain.

In an article for *Forbes*, Ted Sergott (2021) explained how it works:

> An organization runs a job description through its AI platform, and the algorithm will suggest alternatives to biased, gendered, or off-putting language, helping to develop a more balanced job description. Then, when a resume is submitted, the technology strips out elements that might create bias—name, pronouns, photos, address, educational institutions, extracurricular activities, etc. Leading-edge technologies will then use AI to match candidates to the job and create a forced-

rank list of candidates based on skills and experience. Essentially, it provides hiring managers with an unbiased look at how candidates rank based on objective criteria.

You might be thinking that candidate masking can only help so much. After all, won't the hiring manager eventually find out who the candidate is, and judge their personal characteristics then? This is indeed true, and it's the reason candidate masking isn't the only strategy we suggest here.

Use bias-free algorithms

Bias-free algorithms are another key to succeeding with DEI strategies. Equal opportunity algorithms identify unwanted trends in source data to deliver less biased predictions, explain how the algorithm arrived at the predictions, and illustrate to decision-makers how predictions are independent of potentially biased source data. Here's an example. If most scientists in a company are men, and most of the applications are from men, being a man still does not make someone a better scientist. Equal opportunity algorithms make sure that candidate recommendations do not consider gender as a qualification.

Not only does this technology sharply reduce hiring bias, it also increases inclusiveness after an employee is hired because everyone comes in on a level playing field based on their skills and capabilities rather than their pedigree. All employees have the same shot at promotions and networking and mentorship opportunities.

Leverage DEI analytics

DEI analytics finds biases in hiring and also measures the impact of equity policies. These programs show the hiring funnel for each stage and for each diversity category, detecting statistically significant biases. Let's dig a bit deeper. Suppose, for example, that 10 percent of all applicants are members of an under-represented group. This suggests that 10 percent of all hires should also be members of this group, but that's approximate. If 9 percent of hires are members of this group, that might be due to chance. If it's only 5 percent, however, perhaps there is a problem, and an analytics program would flag that 5 percent is very different from 10 percent. In other words, DEI analytics tells you if your hiring outcome is different from what would likely occur due to random chance. It's then up to you to investigate where and why this discrepancy is occurring. Maybe there is a step in the hiring process that turns away a specific group of candidates. For instance, an assessment process may not be accessible enough and therefore adversely impacts candidates living with disabilities. In many cases, unfortunately, the cause is a human making biased decisions. Hopefully, this person just needs awareness and training, but you may need to remove them from a hiring role.

The other side of DEI analytics involves equity policies. We gave the example of a company that has 10 percent of applicants from an under-represented group and assumed that means approximately 10 percent of hires will identify as members of this group—if the hiring process is unbiased. But what if the broader goal of preventing bias demands a different target? Perhaps this group represents 20 percent of the community, and individuals identifying with this group have faced historical disadvantages in applying for a job at the company. Isn't it only fair that the company makes 20 percent of hires from members of this group? In this situation, the company may pursue an equity policy to actively increase the share of applications from this group. A policy like this may be called affirmative action.

Now, we can't tell you what (if any) affirmative action policies are right for your organization. You'd have to consider your local laws, the history of your organization and your society, the expectations of your workforce and your customers, and other relevant factors. But we will say that whatever you do, you need to know if your equity policy is having the intended effect or not. DEI analytics programs can track the effect of equity policies and reveal whether they are doing their job.

Let's compare the importance of measuring equity policies to a familiar subject: vaccine clinical trials. A vaccine must be carefully tested for safety and for efficacy. If you have a new vaccine, just because you think it's going to work based on a computer analysis, and just because you have a logical argument, doesn't mean people will trust it. You need the stats to back you up. You need to prove that the vaccine does what it's supposed to do, and nothing serious that it's not supposed to do. Equity policies must be tested in a similar way. Using DEI analytics, you can find and remove biases that still exist, and lay the foundation for greater fairness in your organization.

Offer self-service talent management to existing employees

Talent management services can include several components that we've already discussed such as upskilling and mobility opportunities. You may define the services that you offer your employees differently. Regardless of how you structure talent management, placing a talent intelligence platform behind your talent management services will create an inclusive basis for those services.

Here's why that's so important. With a skills-based approach to talent management, the standard for career advancement becomes what each employee can do, not who they are. Self-service for talent management allows each employee to explore and make career moves on their own time, without the pressure of a performance review or an HR meeting. Both skills and self-service create a transparent career experience. Every employee finds the available options and knows that the same options are available to others. Each employee sees how the organization will make decisions. When employees can understand how a decision such as promotion is made, they gain confidence in the process.

Finally, your platform should be equally accessible to all employees. Employees with social advantages can't work around it. Mentors can't choose who to coach based on their biases. Important projects can't be staffed at happy hour or by people in the office versus those who work remotely.

Revisit your performance review process

Traditional performance reviews can be problematic from a bias standpoint, and the less standardized they are, the greater the potential for misuse. "When we write particular performance reviews now, we consider if there are words that we're using in reviews that may trigger sensitivity," Jolen Anderson at BNY Mellon told us at our recent Cultivate conference. "For instance, if we're using the word 'aggressive' in a review, is that delivering a message that we want? We prefer managers to be more specific about the exact feedback they're trying to get across to an individual."

Prompt internal hiring managers to inclusive career pathing

Recruiting needs to be balanced with an effective inclusion program to keep a diverse slate of talent in your organization. As much as seminars and training can help, they ignore the big challenge of keeping people long enough to advance in the company. On the internal hiring manager side, talent intelligence platforms provide the same background information about every candidate, because after all, no employee should feel that someone else has more opportunities because they went to the same university as the CEO.

With the right technology supporting DEI throughout the employee lifecycle, your organization can change its entire mindset around careers. Employees will see the presence of opportunity and fair outcomes in action. In time, the expectation of facing bias will be replaced by an expectation of full participation. When this change is achieved, we believe the result will be real inclusion.

As Michael Ross, former CHRO at Visa, shared with us: "We want to use AI to accelerate the opportunity to change the way our organization looks and feels. We want it to enhance our human decision making, we want it to align with the important capabilities we already have and have always known are important. We want our short-term results to feel real. And I think when you use AI inside your various talent processes, you can cast a wider net and make faster progress on delivering what employees want and demand. There's just no time to waste."

SPOTLIGHT ON ONETEN

Collaborative marketplace is bringing together employers, black talent, and upskilling organizations to advance the careers of people of color.

Traditional hiring processes are highly subjective and can have multiple barriers that complicate access to economic opportunities for people of color. Without the ability to assess skills easily and credibly, organizations often fall prey to implicit bias that negatively impacts hiring.

We are making progress, though, especially with black talent. For the last few years, Eightfold has been collaborating with OneTen, a coalition of leading CEOs and their organizations, on an ambitious program to hire, upskill, reskill, and promote one million black individuals without four-year degrees into family-sustaining careers.

OneTen is leading an expert community of black talent, employers, workforce developers, educational institutions, and technology companies to build a career and skills development marketplace that both strengthens existing support systems and disrupts systemic barriers. This marketplace is facilitating the path for black applicants to understand potential career paths, identify needed skills and educational opportunities, and create digital portfolios of the credentials they have acquired through employment, education, or self-directed learning. The program also works to fill skills gaps through accredited learning providers and ultimately match black candidates to optimal jobs.

"The more employers can rely on skills in the hiring process, the less likely bias is to influence hiring outcomes," OneTen CEO Maurice Jones said in a press release. "A skills-first approach opens the aperture of who is included in the talent pool—therefore making it more equitable—and produces better business outcomes with higher performance and retention" (OneTen, 2021).

"By focusing more on skills, we can fast track the career development of black talent so they can more quickly find appropriate education opportunities and high-paying jobs," he added.

The OneTen platform creates consistent tools and processes across three key stakeholders: black talent, organizations that upskill and reskill black talent, and the employers in the OneTen coalition who are looking to hire, promote, and advance black talent.

- **Black talent:** The OneTen platform allows candidates to build out skills-based digital profiles, from which they can create skills maps, take advantage of career planning resources, and track their progress toward upskilling and reskilling for desired jobs or positions. Once courses are completed, OneTen employer members can verify that new skills have been acquired via digital credentials.

- **Talent developers and education institutions:** Organizations focused on cultivating talent benefit from the platform's insights into in-demand skills at major employers. They can also help their students and participants acquire those skills and verify them so they can be more easily connected to promising career opportunities.

- **Member employers:** Employers can use the platform to create and manage job postings, align job postings with trusted industry career frameworks and certifications, and find and engage with talent development organizations and black individuals with the specific skill sets required for available jobs.

Key components of the platform include talent intelligence tools that identify skills and match applicants with jobs they might be interested in, as well as with courses and learning opportunities that will make them more competitive candidates. A Learning Credential Network blockchain provides valued information on the degrees, skills badges, certifications, and credentials that an individual has earned over the course of their career.

"People often respond to criticism about the lack of diversity in their organizations by saying there is a lack of talent. A verifiable jobs and skills ecosystem catered to black talent gives people the opportunity to learn about jobs they might be qualified for while also acquiring the skills they may be lacking," said Merck CEO and OneTen board co-chair Ken Frazier.

Helping on the technology side of this initiative has been very rewarding so far, and we look forward to watching it progress.

Talent intelligence and transitioning veterans

Service members transitioning out of the military have unique skills that can bring value to an employer, but it's often a challenge on both sides (veterans and employers) to understand the potential career trajectories that map back to these skill sets. Talent intelligence can help close the gap, look beyond the words on a resume, and paint a full picture of the skills that transitioning military personnel can bring to the civilian workforce.

"People have this idea that service members are only skilled in combat and make poor employees because they all have PTSD—none of that is true," Justin Constantine told us. He's a retired lieutenant colonel in the Marine Corps and chief business development officer at diversity and inclusion employment platform JobPath Partners. "Veterans make highly skilled and disciplined employees and if you understand how to hire them, that's a steady talent pipeline for you."

If you're familiar with the HR world, you've probably heard of military skills translators. These tools take a person's military experience and try to turn it into something that's useful to employers. You'll find them on some corporate career sites and job boards.

While well intentioned and a good start, they haven't quite done the trick. Corrie Waarum served in the US Air Force, is an active volunteer helping veterans transition to civilian jobs, and has recruited for Amazon and Microsoft. "The tools provided to transitioning veterans in an effort to successfully translate military skills to civilian roles are lackluster at best," she told us.

When service members depart from their time in the military, whether after four years or 30, Transition Assistance Programs (TAPs) match them with counselors to help plan their lives after the military. Our colleague Don Moore talked to a TAP program manager in California. "Military skills translation tends to paint a very one-dimensional picture of people. You're a truck driver in the Army? You could be a truck driver for a private company."

Don Moore is a US Air Force veteran, and a former program manager of himself hiring at L-3 Communications, Gulfstream

Aerospace and General Dynamics. He told us he's an "unabashed champion for career-seeking veterans and spouses, and an evangelist to employers on what they are 'missing.'" He aspires to work with evangelist that can overcome this "you're a truck driver!" mentality.

According to Moore, AI can look closely at the experience of someone who was involved in fuels during their time in the Air Force. While a directly related job may or may not exist in the civilian world, AI can determine how the person's skills could be used—for example, by working for a municipal hazmat team, or on cryogenic or other systems.

Jeff Battinus is a talent acquisition leader working for a series of major healthcare companies. He's also a division commander of the Interpreter Corps of the US Coast Guard auxiliary. Through the years, he has found that efforts to translate military experience into corporate opportunities "are not robust enough."

At Takeda, a multinational biopharmaceutical company, Battinus told us he was looking to hire "metrologists," a profession that involves highly advanced instrument calibration. Even though these roles exist in the US Navy and Air Force, the tools he used to locate veteran candidates weren't useful. Then, Battinus wanted to hire a certain type of water technician. He knew these folks existed as he'd seen them on aircraft carriers and submarines. But again, his sourcing efforts came up empty, so he had to buy lists of people with the right licenses.

This is just basic matching, and talent intelligence can do so much more. Battinus offered the example of an infantry sergeant and the sales skill. "Sergeants are selling all day long, influencing the platoon's morale. Coming into the professional world, they make amazing sales reps."

Along those lines, Tannen Ellis-Graham, a Utah talent acquisition director, said that she was looking for someone to staff an aquarium. "We service fish and kids," she told us. "I was looking for an operations person who could do inventory. The inventory was fish. One of the first resumes I read was from someone from the military who oversaw guns and bullets. Now fish and kids don't mesh with guns and bullets, but I called the guy anyway and learned he'd had to account for every single bullet just like my hire would need to account for every single cricket. AI would have made that association automatically."

Talent intelligence also helps with the translation of soft skills. As Moore said: "People have this stereotype of service members as robots following orders. But AI can look at a military member's experience and assess soft skills like integrating into a team or managing major projects very early in a career. A good recruiter can surface some of that, but this type of platform can go much deeper and rank and stack what a person's most qualified to do."

Recall our earlier discussion of skills adjacencies. Perhaps an Air Force pilot knows technology A but not technology B. Talent intelligence can show an employer that the software (technology B) that the pilot does *not* know is readily learnable by someone who knows technology A.

Or let's say the employer is searching for someone who is comfortable in a "fast-paced environment." A talent intelligence system can spot a soldier who has that comfort level based on their experience, even if their resume doesn't explicitly say anything about being fast-paced.

"The best tool, I've found, is the trained eye of a military recruiter. Oftentimes, veterans can more easily translate relevant skills in a way the business is able to consume," Waarum told us. The goal of talent intelligence is to scale this ability. By scouring thousands upon thousands of military member and veteran profiles, talent intelligence can take the skills of a past or present service member and understand how those skills could be put to (new) work.

Talent intelligence goes a long way in assessing a transitioning service member's true potential and interests. For instance, just because someone worked on satellite equipment in the military doesn't necessarily mean that's what they want to be doing in civilian life. Or perhaps a former military member has gained additional experience since they put away the uniform and would now make a great operations manager, or a capable HR professional. But only talent intelligence applied at a large scale can surface these correlations.

SPOTLIGHT ON MICRON

Computer hardware company used AI to streamline the hiring process for veterans and help them translate their skills to job requirements.

Micron Technology is a world leader in innovating memory and storage solutions that accelerate the transformation of information into intelligence. With more than 40,000 employees in 17 countries, Micron has grown rapidly and was having trouble scaling hiring in a tight labor market.

Specifically, the time to hire was so long that Micron was losing out on top talent. And although the organization had an abundance of applicants, most did not have the desired capabilities or qualifications Micron's hiring managers desperately needed. DEI posed an additional challenge. Micron had committed to increasing diversity hiring year over year but had inefficient mechanisms for bringing in diverse candidates and providing them with the training to successfully perform in available roles.

Micron deployed talent intelligence to reimagine talent management and take an employee-centered approach to career development and inclusion. Once a candidate has created a profile in Micron's portal, the system's algorithms analyze the individual's experience, capabilities, and skills gaps. They then provide insight on potential matches, as well as recommendations to hiring managers for how to further develop that candidate's skills once on board.

Micron's platform now targets transitioning veterans. Mike Thiel, a former Navy paramedic, works on Micron's talent acquisition team and is using machine learning to help veterans translate their skills to the civilian world and assist recruiters in understanding if a military member's skill set aligns to a job's requirements.

Using strategies such as bias-free algorithms and DEI analytics is clearly beneficial to diverse worker outcomes, but we hope this chapter has communicated that the most critical piece is keeping an open mind with respect to the skills that are already present or can be developed in these employees. Talent intelligence gives us the power to do this on a larger scale than we ever have before.

APPLY THE AI

Historically, FutureStrong has not had much luck recruiting and keeping diverse talent. While the organization has positive intentions, few candidates of color make it through FutureStrong's complex hiring process, and once inside the organization, employees of color tend to have shorter tenures and do not progress to management positions at the same pace as Caucasian men.

As FutureStrong's CHRO, what are two or three initial actions you'd take to strengthen your diverse candidate pipeline and/or employee experience, and based on what you've learned in this chapter, how might talent intelligence help?

Chapter summary

- Changing organization-wide behaviors and achieving **DEI goals** starts with **C-level executives** who are emotionally committed to DEI. Practically speaking, building the **inclusion competency** usually includes creating a series of planning sessions for each C-level executive with their direct reports and teams.

- Closed, siloed systems lead to closed, limited thinking that hinders an organization's potential to attain its DEI objectives. Without the benefit of a **single platform**, DEI strategies can take on an optional, not-central role in any organization's current and future direction.

- **Candidate masking** involves blocking unconscious bias by removing all potential pieces of bias—including ethnicity and gender—from resumes so only **objective data points** remain.

- **DEI analytics** illustrates if your hiring outcome is different from what would likely occur due to random chance. It's then up to you to investigate where and why this discrepancy is occurring.

- Traditional hiring processes are highly subjective and can have multiple barriers that complicate access to economic opportunities for **people of color**. Without the ability to assess skills easily and credibly, organizations often fall prey to **implicit bias** that negatively impacts hiring.

- **Transitioning veterans** have unique skills that can bring value to civilian employers, but it's often a challenge to understand the potential career trajectories that map back to these skill sets. Talent intelligence can help close the gap.

6

The government's role in skill development

When Eightfold first came out of stealth mode, we talked more about our goal of finding the right career for everyone in the world. Could we really make this a reality in our lifetime? We were just 30 people back then. How could we possibly solve the employment problem on a global scale?

One sensible approach? Target the largest employers in the world—governments—so they can effect real change. We knew this would be a challenge. In most countries and regions, governments are slow and bureaucratic. When governments are trying to hire candidates, the deck is stacked against them because everything—from getting a job description approved to negotiating compensation—takes a very long time. Due to this pace of entrenched systems, governments naturally attract people who excelled in a given role five years ago.

Kamal had the chance to talk with a major general at the White House. He lamented that he needed the same technical talent as Amazon, but the government pay scale is a fraction of what the private sector can afford. He was also having trouble cultivating the right talent within his ranks: entry-level recruits were too green, mid-tier officers weren't loyal, and senior leaders were out of touch. He needed a platform that could help yesterday.

Ashu and Kamal figured that if there was a two-year gestation period before they could sell talent intelligence to governments, they'd better get started. While proceeding through the required steps, Eightfold kept raising money to improve the technology. The first government customer was the US state of Indiana, and we used that case to convince the US state of New York, which is larger than most countries, to come on board. Then we were off and running!

We will never forget what a woman in New York told us after the state implemented talent intelligence to scour for potential: "I realized that I'm more than my resume when the system recommended all sorts of jobs I hadn't thought about. For the first time, I really felt appreciated for what I'm doing."

Last year, the technology analyst firm IDC predicted that around now, 60 percent of government agencies would be deploying AI-enabled technologies to recruit, train, and retain key personnel (O'Brien, 2021). Could governments be adopting technology such as talent intelligence faster than their private-sector counterparts? This might in fact be the case, and, as we've alluded to, the urgency comes in part from desperation.

Unbeatable offers from private-sector employers, the retirement of baby boomers, skills shortages, and evolving employee expectations are fueling a talent crisis that has become one of the biggest challenges facing public-sector employers.

During the 2008 recession, governments laid off and furloughed employees in huge numbers, and then did so again during the early days of Covid-19. In the United States, now that the American Rescue Plan has kicked in, public-sector HR departments have gotten the green light to add positions. The trouble is finding people to fill those jobs.

Each year, the US Center for State and Local Government Excellence (SLGE) produces a *State and Local Workforce* report. As part of a 2021 *Governing* article, SLGE senior research analyst Gerald Young told author Carl Smith that one of the key differences between the 2021 survey and the one conducted following the 2008 recession was a dramatic shift in retirement trends (Mission Square Research Institute, 2021).

In 2009, 44 percent of respondents said that eligible staff were planning to postpone retirement, but in 2021 only 2 percent said this. In 2021, 38 percent said retirement-eligible staff were planning to accelerate retirement, compared with 12 percent in 2009 (Smith, 2021).

"This is placing an additional burden on organizations who have difficulty recruiting anyway," Young said. Moreover, the Silver Tsunami has not reached its peak. More than half of those surveyed believe that the biggest wave will come in the next few years.

More than half of SLGE survey participants reported difficulty filling positions in healthcare, policing, corrections, engineering, and skilled trades. Carl Smith wrote that some of the recruiting problems may be aftereffects of the recent racial justice turmoil, others the result of competition with the private sector.

Smith interviewed Karen Niparko, executive director of the Office of Human Resources for the city and county of Denver, in the US state of Colorado. She commented that while a shortage of law enforcement applicants is not new, recent societal events will make it even harder to fill these roles. "People are becoming reluctant and a little nervous about becoming police officers," she told Smith. "In some states, a police officer can be personally sued for behavior on the job, and that scares people."

Not surprisingly, governments can't bring in IT workers fast enough either. In the SLGE survey, six in 10 jurisdictions said the number of positions they had for IT employees was greater than the number of people who applied for them. Nearly two-thirds said the same thing about wages, competition, and workplace culture for engineering jobs.

The Centre for Equity Studies' 2021 *India Exclusion Report*, a collaborative effort involving institutions and individuals working with a shared notion of social and economic equity, justice, and rights, reflected many of the same concerns about viable government employment in that country (Centre for Equity Studies, 2021).

"Since so many essential services must be provided by governments, and it is impossible to provide them without employing people to do so, the extent of public employment is a useful indicator of the coverage and quality of public services," the report said. "By this indicator, India performs very poorly: public employment in India is only one-tenth of that in Norway, only 15 percent of that in Brazil, and much less than a third of that in China."

As in many places, government vacancies in India have increased in recent years, which is having a major impact on the public services that cannot be delivered without people.

Technology is, of course, an essential part of the solution for confronting this crisis. "Agencies need to accelerate their digital transformation efforts now to retain top talent and attract new talent to fill the gap," wrote Jonathan Benett, technical director for digital government solutions at Adobe, in an article for *Government Executive* (Benett, 2020).

Public agencies need every edge they can get in the talent marketplace. "Without a doubt, the public sector starts at a disadvantage and can now be in danger of lagging even farther behind the eight ball on recruiting," Jennifer Marie Rocks, managing director at Deloitte, wrote in a recent research piece (Long, 2021).

Talent intelligence can help public agencies stay competitive in the war for talent in several ways, including reducing the time to hire and broadening the candidate talent pool. In the rest of this chapter, we'll discuss talent attraction and retention in the public sector, the government's role in digital upskilling, and how talent intelligence can be used to address government employment challenges.

Talent attraction and retention in the public sector

Public-sector employers are known for taking a long time to bring on new employees. According to data gathered by the Partnership for Public Service and Boston Consulting Group, it takes the US federal government about 98 days to onboard a new hire, which is more than double the time it takes a private-sector employer (Partnership for Public Service and BCG, 2020).

A shorter time to hire is critical for attracting high-quality candidates. As John Sullivan, professor of management at San Francisco State University, said in *HR Daily Advisor*, "in-demand candidates are the first to drop out or ghost in frustration" (Blazejak, 2019).

Before they are even hired, candidates expect prospective employers to show them a map of their career with the organization and how management will support them along that path. "The feeling that there's a progression and a trajectory to their career makes a big difference for people," said Rivka Liss-Levinson, director of research at MissionSquare Research Institute, in an article for *SHRM* by Mike Ramsey. "Unfortunately, identifying those career paths is an area where many public agencies fall short, and it costs them in terms of talent acquisition and retention" (Ramsey, 2020).

And once in a role, public-sector employees seek the power of movement. A key part of career autonomy is the chance to apply for desirable internal job openings. "No one wants to remain in a stationary position for years on end, especially when they can see the potential for growth elsewhere," wrote Evelyn Long, cofounder and editor-in-chief at *Renovated*, in an article for *Training Journal* (Long, 2021).

But outdated leader mindsets present a huge challenge to this approach. Many believe public-sector career paths should be hierarchical and based on performance rather than skills. They don't see the potential of their employees to succeed in new types of roles, so they hire from the outside.

When it comes to retention, work flexibility is just as much at play in the public sector as in the private one. According to Carl Smith in *Governing*, more than half of government agencies now offer regular telework for eligible positions (Smith, 2021).

Recall that Karen Niparko is the executive director of the Office of Human Resources for the city and county of Denver. She expects full- or part-time remote work to become the norm for jobs that don't require in-person contact with the public. "I don't believe we'll ever go back to the way it was pre-Covid," she said. "We learned that we could get a lot of work done, that we could innovate, and improve processes in many cases."

Coming out of the pandemic, a great majority of public-sector organizations (75 percent) gave more employees access to work practices such as flexible weekly schedules and work hours, and 72 percent increased the range of such options.

Of course, how flexible public-sector organizations can be depends on the services that can be delivered online. At the state and local level, for instance, if your driver's license renewal policy indicates that a customer must visit a Department of Motor Vehicles in person, you will need an employee who is physically there to assist them.

The government's role in digital upskilling

Technology advances and the expansion of virtual services are redefining the jobs that organizations need to fill, and the training employees need to hold these jobs.

In many ways, the Covid-19 pandemic exposed the flaws in unemployment systems. Around the world, once an unemployment claim is processed, the government's work is done. We have a re-employment system that relies on displaced workers' ability to search and interpret vaguely worded job descriptions and to self-assess their own fit to roles.

For the unemployed, finding a job is often a search problem. There are plenty of jobs out there but figuring out the positions that are right for you is another matter. And anyone who has ever done a job search knows it's a broken, frustrating, and time-consuming process.

Yet many governments subsidize this inefficient system, paying millions of dollars weekly until their residents discover the right job. Leaders are only now realizing that if they can optimize the job-matching system and train their populations in desirable skill areas, they can quickly find people the right employment opportunities and reduce time on unemployment and benefit obligations.

In 2018, China was one of the first nations to develop an action plan for the incorporation of AI into higher education curricula, forecasting a shortage of 300,000 AI-trained employees in the coming years. The Ministry of Education's plan identified three major issues in China's current AI talent pool: a significant mismatch between skills and jobs, a short supply of highly skilled AI talent, and a regional imbalance of AI talent.

At the national and local levels, China pledged to build 100 "AI+X" models to nurture AI talents in specific fields, to build 50 AI colleges, AI research centers, or cross-collaborative research centers, and to introduce AI in primary and secondary schools.

In a similar vein, the UK government published a National AI Strategy, which aims to create a progressive and pro-innovation regulatory environment to enable UK businesses in all sectors and regions to benefit from AI adoption and allow them to compete internationally.

The UK government's strategy involves developing, attracting, and training the best people to build and use AI technologies in the UK by: a) granting additional government-backed fellowships and scholarships; b) revising immigration rules to encourage top AI talent from around the globe to come to the UK; and c) delivering additional (and more relevant) training to the existing workforce, including those who would not have traditionally engaged with AI.

In Australia, the federal government is developing an AU$10 million data tool that provides real-time information about Australia's regional and local area workforce, skills, and labor market. "Data at a regional level will provide us with a better picture of the supply and demand, assist with workforce planning, and mean that both business and government will be able to focus on better matching of skills and training to local needs," said Stuart Robert, the minister responsible for Australia's workforce, in an article by Campbell Kwan for *ZDNet* (Kwan, 2021).

The Australian government is also allocating AU$20 million over the next four years to fast-track skills assessments for occupations with skills shortages, waiving fees, and giving extra benefits to migrants.

The initiative also provides free employability assessments and support for migrants working at a skill level below their qualifications. Other measures include adding funding for industry-focused short courses at universities and piloting novel approaches to accelerating qualification completion times.

Upskilling and reskilling government employees themselves is a separate issue, and many are concerned that worldwide government agencies do not have the skills they need to maintain an effective mid-21st-century workforce.

As an example, in 2021, the US National Security Commission on Artificial Intelligence (NSCAI) issued a report proposing how the US Department of Defense and the intelligence community could be "AI-ready" by 2025 (NSCAI, 2021).

The Commission was convened in response to the fear that the US armed forces will lose their competitive military-technical advantage within the next decade. Monitoring battlefields, understanding adversarial strategies, and augmenting human service member perception and decision-making capabilities are all areas that can be strengthened by AI.

The report provided the US Congress with 100-plus recommendations for the country to stay ahead of AI competitors like China. NSCAI chairman Eric Schmidt, the former CEO of Google, told lawmakers that there's a "huge talent deficit that will only worsen if defense and civilian agencies don't develop career pathways for rising talent to stay in government service."

According to Jory Heckman, who covered the 2021 hearing for *Federal News Network*, Schmidt agreed with other commissioners that DoD and civilian agencies could probably reskill a decent portion of the current workforce into AI-focused jobs. But until agencies figure out a way to identify employees with the skills and aptitude needed to succeed in AI-focused jobs, Schmidt said those employees will remain underutilized (Heckman, 2021).

Commissioner Mignon Clyburn, a former commissioner at the Federal Communications Commission, recommended that the DoD create an emerging technology certification process. "Service members would earn these certifications by serving in non-critical emerging technology billets, fellowships with industry and academia, and through industry certification courses," wrote Heckman about the proposal.

The Commission also discussed plans for the US Digital Service Academy, a university modeled after the military service academies. Students would agree to five-year terms in government service after graduating, and several university partners have signed on to facilitate the academy.

Employment is the backbone of our society and everyone deserves the right job. The pandemic forced government leaders to take a hard look at their existing systems and realize that it's time for a change. Technological innovations over the last decade have provided powerful tools for governments around the world to overcome employment and training barriers. A modern system that identifies local needs, enables self-service, reduces time on unemployment, and reduces underemployment through upskilling and reskilling is in everyone's best interest.

SPOTLIGHT ON THE US STATE OF NEW YORK
US state taught its employers to decrease the emphasis on job titles and improve their analysis of candidate potential.

New York state is one of the most populous in the United States and has a larger population than most countries in the world. Following the Covid-19 pandemic, New York's Department of Labor focused on getting citizens back to work and providing upskilling and reskilling opportunities for sustainable careers going forward. There was an urgent need: in 2020 and 2021, the state paid nearly $100 billion in unemployment to nearly five million New Yorkers. That's 45 years of benefits in just 17 months.

Many New Yorkers, a good portion of them women, had to leave their jobs to care for their children and elders during the pandemic. These citizens were now re-evaluating whether they wanted to go back to the same job or strike out in a different direction. The Department of Labor recognized the opportunity to shift the thinking and remove the traditional barriers to enter certain fields.

However, a fundamental misalignment existed. New York's businesses complained they couldn't find skilled workers, while the workers said they didn't have the right training to work in those organizations.

The Department of Labor wanted to ensure that every New Yorker has a chance to participate in meaningful work. It started by looking at skills as a language that everyone needs to get better at speaking. The Department began educating the population about the importance of lifelong learning and seeking additional training when one's current industry is changing, or one wishes to enter a new industry.

In consulting with employers across the state, the Department of Labor noticed that two skill areas were in hot demand—digital literacy and professional soft skills. It then provided free access to online learning repository Coursera and SUNY Online, the state university system's learning platform, and zeroed in on those skills.

Department of Labor Commissioner Roberta Reardon also encouraged employers to stop talking about job titles. "It's not that you need to hire a receptionist, it's that you need to hire someone with the skill to manage the people in your office. We must talk about what people do, not about the credentials they have, and we need to help workers own and articulate their skills," she said at our recent Cultivate conference.

Next, the Department of Labor built a virtual career services portal that incorporated talent intelligence to help over a million New Yorkers with their searches. "AI allows us to scale. It allows us to reach out to individuals and answer their questions without them having to sit in a career center with a counselor, one-on-one," Reardon said.

The portal addresses the needs of both entry-level and skilled workers, and provides every individual the ability to upload resumes, browse their top job matches, apply for positions relevant to their skills, and explore training opportunities to step up in their careers.

Talent intelligence in government employment

Talent intelligence tools enable hiring teams to onboard candidates more quickly, keeping public agencies in the running for the top candidates. They also create larger talent pools from which public-sector employers can pull candidates to fill roles. Anyone with a profile in the system—current employees, alumni, external candidates that have applied, past applicants—can be tapped as a potential hire based on the skills and goals in their profiles.

Employers increase their likelihood of finding the right person for the job with a broader talent pool, because government employment is often not top of mind for top talent. So instead of passively waiting to see who applies for an open role, employers can actively recruit from a variety of fruitful sources.

For local governments that are competing for talent with other municipalities, a broader pool plays a large role in their success. "One of the biggest threats to our communities is leaving jobs unfilled, because if we do, the jobs will go somewhere else. There are companies looking to relocate here, to bring their jobs here, and we've needed a better mousetrap to capture the required skills. We must be able to say that we have people who are job ready," said Mike Barnes, chief workforce officer at the Indiana Department of Workforce Development, at our Cultivate conference.

As we briefly mentioned back in Chapter 1, the US Department of Defense (DoD) has developed Gig Eagle to identify talent in the National Guard and reserve forces that could be utilized for special projects in the DoD. On the DoD's website, Scott Sumner, technical project manager, said that there's a lot of talent out there that the DoD could be using but is not aware of. "Reservists in their civilian jobs might be working on cloud computing, software engineering, cybersecurity or any number of other in-demand skills. The problem is that the DoD has no way to find them or to know that those skills even exist," he said (Vergun, 2021).

Gig Eagle's matching system is powered by talent intelligence. The platform considers skill preferences and biographical information that the Guard member or reservist enters into the app. The AI algorithm notes words that indicate or infer a particular talent or skill. A hiring manager from the DoD then receives a ranked list of possible candidates.

The data mined by platforms like Gig Eagle is also used to build employee profiles and career maps so employees (or Guard members or reservists, in the case of Gig Eagle) have autonomy over their direction with the organization. Through a talent intelligence system, employees can see the skills they need to develop to move further along their career paths.

Talent intelligence increases the visibility of job opportunities for those who are already employed by the institution. Anybody can match their employee profile against a job description to see if they would be a good fit and then apply for the position. The technology also eliminates the need for employees to ask permission from managers to apply for different positions, which is a common barrier that keeps employees from advancing in government agencies.

With more candidates applying, public-sector employers are better equipped to hire workers who will have a long-term future with the agency. This, along with the ability to provide employees with options for their future, allows public institutions to effectively address the talent crisis that continues to plague them.

Finally, most governments are concerned with labor participation and keeping citizens in the area. "Talent intelligence helps individuals figure out how to transfer their skills and take advantage of options they never saw for themselves," said Mike Barnes at Cultivate. "When I work with citizens one-on-one, they might say something like: 'But I just was a machine operator.' People don't think of themselves in terms of their skills, but we can use talent intelligence to translate all the experiences they've had in-job to the skills that are needed now. And this leads to an overall better labor participation rate."

SPOTLIGHT ON THE US STATE OF INDIANA

US state used talent intelligence and equal opportunity algorithms to uncover hidden capabilities among the region's workers.

The Indiana Department of Workforce Development (DWD) is responsible for innovating and invigorating Indiana's economic future by providing WorkOne career centers, unemployment insurance, labor market information, regional workforce strategies and professional training.

Through these services, DWD is developing a workforce in which Indiana employers flourish and businesses outside the state want to relocate there.

In December 2020, Indiana's unemployment rate was 4.3 percent. While lower than the national rate of 6.7 percent at the time, it was still higher than the 3.2 percent of the previous year.

In response, the DWD unveiled the Hoosier Talent Network, a job-matching and career-planning platform powered by talent intelligence to help job seekers quickly find the right opportunities in the right locations. By better understanding individual skills and capabilities, the Hoosier Talent Network unlocks opportunities based on a candidate's unique potential.

Job seekers can upload their resume or quickly create a profile of work history, skills, and hobbies. After completing the profile, individuals can view open roles and receive email notifications with suggestions for jobs that align with their specific skills and experiences. These matches will be a result of the information they self-reported in their profile and the inferences that the platform has made using its expansive analysis of different career paths.

"In addition to gathering data on job seekers' current skill sets, the technology provides insight into how they can expand their capabilities. If certain skills appear to be missing from a user's profile, the Talent Network will suggest skills that could easily be learned to further expand career possibilities," wrote Julia Edinger in an article about the program for *Government Technology* (Edinger, 2021).

"In the coming years, the skill sets needed by employers are likely to transform as things like new technology, remote work, and automation are considered. The emphasis on helping match job seekers with easily learnable skills is one way to combat this impending transformation."

The job openings posted on the website cover a wide variety of occupations and skill levels. But the Hoosier Talent Network is not just for job seekers. Hiring organizations can also use the technology to get matched with all types of potential workers. "One thing that makes this platform effective is the use of Equal Opportunity Algorithms to prevent bias," Edinger said. "The platform can mask the profiles, letting employers focus on the candidates and their capabilities rather than other factors that are not relevant."

At the time of the Hoosier Talent Network launch, approximately 135,000 Indiana residents were out of work. "One person becoming employed at a sustainable wage has a big ripple impact throughout the economy," said Mike Barnes, chief workforce officer at the Indiana Department of Workforce Development. "It lowers poverty rates, it raises education levels, and it raises diversity and equity within our communities. AI can be the equalizer in helping people achieve opportunities that they didn't see as possible for themselves."

Barnes shared the story of Linda, a 51-year-old from southern Indiana. Linda never completed her high school diploma and had worked in a variety of low-wage, low-skill environments. Currently a convenience store cashier, Linda heard about the Talent Network. She wanted to change direction, so she logged in to see the skill profile for a healthcare worker.

"The system put Linda in touch with her local adult education provider, and together they worked on her high school equivalency and a certified nursing certificate," Barnes explained. "Now she has a new job and her eyes on becoming an LPN. When she emailed us, she said that she never realized she was as smart as she apparently is, or that she had this much potential."

Talent intelligence helps public agencies reduce their time to hire and broaden their candidate pools in a multitude of ways, while simultaneously providing opportunities to upskill and redeploy large numbers of citizens who have the potential to do great work for their towns, cities, countries, and the world.

APPLY THE AI

FutureStrong is experiencing a data science skills shortage and would like to partner with the public sector to pipeline local data scientists into the company. The government labor organization has asked how it might help locate and train citizens who have either experimented with data science or, based on their existing skills, have the potential to become data scientists.

What do you suggest to the commissioner, and how could you work with the government to make any technology implementations a reality?

Chapter summary

- Talent intelligence can help public agencies stay competitive in the war for talent in several ways, including **reducing the time to hire** and **broadening the candidate talent pool**.

- Once in a role, public-sector employees seek the **power of movement**. A key part of career autonomy is the chance to apply for desirable internal job openings, but **outdated leader mindsets** present a huge challenge to this approach.

- Coming out of the pandemic, a great majority of public-sector organizations gave more employees access to work practices such as **flexible** weekly schedules and work hours, but how flexible public-sector organizations can be depends on the **services that can be delivered online**.

- Public-sector leaders are realizing that if they can optimize a **job-matching** system, they can quickly find people the right employment opportunities and **reduce time on unemployment** and benefit obligations.

- **Upskilling and reskilling** government employees themselves has captured the attention of leaders and committees worldwide, as many are concerned that agencies do not have the skills they need to maintain an effective mid-21st-century workforce.

- Talent intelligence platforms give public-sector employers the ability to not only show **existing employees** where they can go in their careers within the organization but also help them get there with **customized training recommendations and resources**.

7

Talent intelligence and industry-specific labor shortages

The financial services industry has captured Kamal and Ashu's attention because it is being disrupted before our eyes. Your local bank has hooked up with Zelle (a digital payments network) and Fidelity (an investment management company) is saying you can have cryptocurrency in your retirement plan. Kamal's gardener is the only person he knows who still wants a physical check, and Alexandra's Generation Z children have never seen one.

Some people are not as interested in owning a home with a mortgage because it ties them to a particular place, and many don't want to be beholden to a bank for any reason. The question of "what is money?" is up for debate as transactions occur through an ever-increasing number of channels, and the younger generations especially are here for it.

Kamal is fascinated by the financial services industry's investment in building the infrastructure to support this transformation. These organizations need talent to help shape what you need money for, and where and how you can spend it, and then build essential systems to support this innovation.

Throughout this book, we've been discussing the problem of global labor shortages. But all labor shortages aren't created equal. According to Andrew Van Dam's article for the *Washington Post*, while economists and policymakers debate whether the economy at large faces a shortage of qualified workers, data shows that it's really a handful of sectors having the most trouble finding employees, including financial services (Van Dam, 2021).

Van Dam interviewed *Indeed* economist Nick Bunker, who said that there in fact isn't a broad worker shortage. "When you have a shortage in the market, you're doing your best to get supply by paying more for it, but nothing's happening," Bunker said. "A true worker shortage means that businesses see little response despite an aggressive search for workers."

The *Post* sought to answer the question of the industries where workers were truly in short supply. It analyzed US federal wage and employment data from hundreds of industries and pinpointed those where employers paid higher wages but still didn't attract new workers. These sectors included manufacturing, utilities, and business and financial services.

In industries like these, "companies have already snapped up the most obvious candidates," said Van Dam. This means that employers must search harder for employees, and perhaps think about recruitment a bit differently.

In 2022, the Eightfold team gathered insights from our global talent intelligence platform to analyze business trends in three industries and determine how labor shortages can be solved through skill matching and development. The rest of this chapter will take a deep dive into the business transformation and workforce realities of telecommunications, semiconductor manufacturing, and financial services.

Telecommunications

The telecommunications industry is experiencing a period of mass transformation, especially as leaders make headway in delivering on the promise of these seamless, high-quality, safe connections through 5G and other new offerings.

And 5G isn't the only emerging trend at the top of the agenda. The growing importance of edge computing, AI and big data, IoT (Internet of Things), cloud computing, software-defined networking, and Open Radio Access Networks (RANs) means new offerings for telecom. Innovation in IoT, for example, is introducing smart grid automation and smart cities, smart home devices, monitoring systems, and autonomous vehicles to consumers' lives.

Jennifer Tracy, vice president of talent attraction and acquisition at Spectrum, told us that the increased sophistication of the average customer is impacting the industry's approach to talent.

"Customers today are much more likely to install equipment themselves, leading to evolving responsibilities for field tech roles. What you need now is the technical know-how to troubleshoot with a customer," she said.

Building and improving these capabilities across 5G, edge computing, AI and big data, IoT, cloud computing, and Open RAN requires a significant investment in new technologies, processes, and skills that are already in short supply.

"5G is here already and 10G is right behind," said Tracy. "That's just the natural progression of technology and the business that we're in. You have to stay current."

Staying current involves proper workforce planning with four key talent groups. In a typical telecom organization, about 45 percent of employees are customer-facing, housed within the sales, retail, customer service, and call center functions.

About 30 percent work on the technical side, including functions such as product management, software development, IT, and analytics. Approximately 15 percent work in core operations functions like design, implementation, and maintenance of networks. And finally, 10 percent are housed in administration and support departments, including HR, finance, accounting, legal, and supply chain.

Eightfold assessed a variety of roles and skills across telecom organizations to determine whether they have the talent in place to be truly innovative. We learned that due to factors like automation and new business models, many of the most familiar roles within telecoms are either stable or declining in prevalence.

A stark 33 percent of the top network engineering and operations roles are declining in prevalence. Telecoms have a significant number of network and field technicians, but these jobs are also declining in prevalence. However, organizations often lack enough construction managers and cybersecurity engineers to address demand.

In the customer-facing divisions, the most common roles are all declining—sales representatives and retail sales consultants, for instance. Within technology and analytics, the role of the IT technician is also declining. In business support, administrative assistant roles are on the decline.

We found a similar situation when we looked at skills. Many of the most common skills are declining in usage, including commercial skills like customer service and sales management, as well as basic technology and word processing skills. In the last 10 years, telecoms have experienced a major shift in the skills necessary for a variety of roles.

The changing role of a network engineer is a prime example. In 2010, the top rising skills included several that weren't on the rising skill list for 2020, such as C# and MATLAB. In 2020, top rising skills for network engineers included Python, Amazon Web Services, 4G/5G, cloud computing, and Juniper switches. None of these was on the 2010 list.

Software engineering also saw a dramatic change. In 2010, top rising skills included Scrum, AJAX, Jira, and Apache Maven. In 2020, top rising skills included Docker, Git, HTML5, react.js, and others not on the list a decade prior.

Telecom organizations have the ability to build out some skills areas more than others. While the industry is poised to improve its capabilities for cloud and edge computing and Big Data, our analysis identified low workforce readiness in areas such as 5G and Open RAN.

By looking at historical capability trends from the emergence of LTE and HSPA, for example, we can see that telecom organizations have a short window of one to two years to build 5G capabilities. Providers must accelerate 5G expansion and prepare for the 6G capabilities that are necessary for technologies like the metaverse to take shape.

So right now, telecom organizations are behind, and to quickly catch up, they should do three things that by now are familiar to you: 1) upskill and reskill their current workforce; 2) calibrate roles with future skills; and 3) hire for potential.

Upskilling, reskilling, and cross-skilling bridge the gap between declining and rising skills. Take business support roles. An employee may know PeopleSoft, GAAP standards, and data entry, all of which are on the decline. Depending on their role, they might add skills such as social media management, digital marketing, and employee engagement, which are all rising and in demand.

Other employees with retail sales, store management, and inventory control skills can add digital sales, SaaS, and strategic partnership skills to future-proof their roles.

This is where our concept of adjacent skills comes in. With AI capabilities now available to draw actionable insights from data, we can see patterns. Who is capable of learning what? If you know skill A, might you be able to pick up skill B?

Edge computing, for example, is a future skill in the telecommunications world. Adjacent skills include cloud computing, LTE, and wireless technologies. People with wireless tech skills are in a good position to move into a future-ready role in edge computing.

Taking this a step further, we can identify career paths for telecom employees in which they move from declining roles to in-demand ones based on skill adjacencies.

For instance, the skill set of a network technician overlaps with that of a cybersecurity engineer. If a network technician chooses to explore the cybersecurity engineer career path, they can use existing routing and troubleshooting skills and learn new skills like disaster recovery.

Telecom organizations can also build a workforce of tomorrow by calibrating roles with the skills of the future. As one example, we might envision what a future network engineer role will look like. A recruiter might seek talent with current top skills, such as network engineering, as well as emerging skills like Python and 5G. The recruiter could include rising skills at the most forward-thinking companies, such as Cisco Nexus and Git.

For a future-ready Big Data engineering role, calibration might involve current top skills like Hadoop, quickly growing skills like Amazon Web Services, and emerging skills like Python and data science that are most prevalent in the workforces of fast-growing, highly innovative organizations.

Talent intelligence makes role calibration much easier, and it can also lend a hand in telecom organizations' third strategy, which is hiring for potential. As we've talked about, hiring for potential allows organizations to tap into a significantly larger pool of qualified talent, and it isn't done nearly enough.

Take a future skill like Python. Looking for candidates with Python skills, an employer would encounter a pool of about a million people. But when recruiters consider candidates with adjacent skills and use talent intelligence to identify who is most capable of picking up Python quickly—the pool doubles to two million. Adjacent skills include C++, algorithms, Java, R, and data structures.

Expanding the talent pool by considering potential, in addition to calibration and upskilling and reskilling, will ultimately help telecom companies build a workforce with the right skills to tackle emerging challenges.

SPOTLIGHT ON ERICSSON

Swedish telecommunications company used talent intelligence to uncover hidden candidates and make decisions about how and where to look for in-demand telecommunications skills.

The 145-year-old Ericsson is involved in a variety of cutting-edge technologies, including autonomous vehicles. It's also using talent intelligence for the acquisition and management of the tens of thousands of people it hires annually.

Sasha Worthington heads up the team responsible for transforming the end-to-end Ericsson hiring journey across the globe. If you had to boil down the goal, she said, it's to "operate in a very smart way by accessing the best people on the market as quickly as possible. We need to make it much quicker and easier for our recruiters and our hiring managers."

To accomplish that, Worthington said, "we're really embracing AI in any way we can across the People function." That embrace begins with talent acquisition because the telecoms market is so competitive.

Ericsson has already found value in better matching because talent intelligence can infer skills a candidate may have left out of their resume. Ericsson can get 1,000 applicants for one role and it's difficult for a human recruiter to examine each resume closely and read between the lines. "No longer are recruiters needing to troll through all of those candidates to find the best applicants," Worthington said. "The best ones are floated to the top. And they're not just the best ones based on the skills that we require. Our talent pool is widening and we're finding candidates that we may not have previously found, which is powerful."

Ericsson will now turn its attention to better understanding the skills of its 100,000-plus workforce. "We want to make it very simple and easy for employees to own and manage their own careers," she said. "Next year we're going to focus on enabling our employees to identify opportunities across the globe and really start to reskill and upskill."

Ericsson's hiring managers actively use their talent intelligence platform to inform their decisions. Managers know whether they must go externally for skills, or whether the workforce has the right skills to hire internally.

As for Ericsson's employees, they use the platform to find new roles within the company, including roles they hadn't even considered previously but were suggested by the system. These recommendations are also tied into learning so employees can take any coursework necessary for a new role.

Semiconductor manufacturing

In 1990, the United States and Europe together produced over 75 percent of semiconductors worldwide. Today, between them they produce less than 25 percent, while China is en route to become the world's largest producer by 2030 (Fitch and Santiago, 2020).

Building new fabrication plants or "fabs" comes with several challenges. The cost of a new plant is high—from \$12–\$15 billion over the course of two years—and fabs cannot be created in a vacuum. "New fabs rely on a connection to the global [integrated circuit] ecosystem, a highly effective collaborative knowledge network that has taken 50 years to build," Jim Koonmen, executive vice president of applications at ASML, said (Duffy, 2021).

To support the building of new manufacturing plants, Intel recently announced the creation of Intel Foundry Services, which provides manufacturing capacity for semiconductors within the United States and Europe.

"We need enough new, global semiconductor manufacturing capacity to avoid depending on any single country or company for these crucial products," Intel CEO Pat Gelsinger wrote at the time of the announcement (Gelsinger, 2021).

Building fabs is only the first step to bolstering semiconductor manufacturing capacity, as many Asian countries have already discovered. "Part of [Taiwan's and South Korea's] success over the last 20 years is due to supportive government policies and access to skilled labor forces," said Neil Campling, head of technology, media, and telecoms research at Mirabaud Securities (Kharpal, 2021).

Although some governments have promised funding, for example via the US Build Back Better Act in the United States, growing a capable workforce mostly lies in the hands of semiconductor manufacturers themselves.

Creating new semiconductor manufacturing capacity would be difficult enough if the work were limited to building new plants. But semiconductor companies also face disruption of the work itself, as changes wrought by automation create higher demand for certain skills and roles while pushing others toward obsolescence.

In our recent analysis, Eightfold found that three main role groups are necessary to run a fabrication plant successfully:

- **Logistics and support:** Accounting for only about 15 percent of plant staff, these workers nonetheless face outsized challenges as they procure materials, maintain facilities, and interact with corporate and business services.

- **Production engineering:** Tasks performed by this group include designing, running, testing, and upgrading systems and processes. About 20–25 percent of fab workers fall in this category.

- **Production operations:** Currently the largest of the three groups, workers here run, monitor, and troubleshoot production equipment. They account for 60–65 percent of workers in most fabs.

The populations of these categories are already in flux. Innovations in manufacturing are decreasing the number of production operation workers required in some fabrication plants, while placing increased pressure on workers to learn and use the skills required in production engineering and logistics.

The rise of new forms of design and manufacturing software, for example, is pushing workers to learn new systems and to retire skills related to older systems, software, and programming languages.

As job roles in semiconductor manufacturing fluctuate, workers' daily tasks demand more flexibility. A 2021 White House report on US semiconductor supply chains noted that "resilient production requires quick problem-solving, driven by the knowledge, leadership, and full engagement of people on the factory floor" (The White House, 2021).

As in the telecommunications industry, the semiconductor manufacturing industry can deploy talent intelligence to better understand the commonalities and interrelationships between various job roles and skill sets. This technology offers new insights to hiring managers, who can then focus on candidates with the capacity to learn quickly and grow into a necessary role.

Our analysis found that many semiconductor operational roles are declining in prevalence. However, these declining roles share essential skills with roles that are steady or increasing in prevalence. For example:

- **Manufacturing technicians** share various skills with process engineers and reliability engineers.

- **Equipment technicians** may transition easily to equipment specialists or instrumentation and controls engineers, given the similarity of skills required.

- **Electronic technicians** have several skills in common with electrical maintenance and embedded systems engineers.

Specific skills within each role also have adjacent skills. Remember that proficiency in an adjacent skill provides a worker with the familiarity and background required to learn a new target skill efficiently. Workers who possess the context provided by adjacent skills also can think through problems from a new perspective. Handy skills adjacencies for semiconductor fabrication include:

- **Process automation:** Skill in process automation is closely related to skills in process control and process engineering.

- **Continuous improvement:** Workers with skills in lean manufacturing, 5S, and Six Sigma possess adjacent skills to continuous improvement.

- **Python:** Skill in Python is adjacent to skill in C++ and Java, as well as skill in designing algorithms.

Mapping adjacent roles and skills provides two essential opportunities for semiconductor manufacturers staffing fabrication plants. First, it allows them to reskill and upskill employees, creating career growth opportunities by guiding workers' existing skill sets into new but related domains. Second, it allows employers to broaden their talent search by including candidates whose adjacent skills will facilitate quick mastery and innovation.

SPOTLIGHT ON TAIWAN SEMICONDUCTOR MANUFACTURING COMPANY

The world's largest contract chipmaker is addressing supply chain issues by relying on talent intelligence instead of traditional qualifications like a degree or an industry specialty.

With 51 percent of the global chip market, Taiwan Semiconductor Manufacturing Company (TSMC) is bringing together a mix of current employees and new hires to run a $12 billion chipmaking plant it is building in the US state of Arizona.

According to an article in *Nikkei Asia*, the new plant will create more than 1,600 direct jobs and thousands of indirect jobs for the semiconductor ecosystem. Many TSMC suppliers such as Marketech International Corp., a semiconductor facility builder, as well as leading chip material provider Entegris, have indicated plans to expand in Arizona (Ting-Fang and Li, 2020).

Per chairman Mark Liu, a task force of current employees and managers with experience in developing and producing five-nanometer chips is helping to get operations off the ground. Five-nanometer chips are the most advanced in the world and are used in the latest iPhone 12 range and Mac processors.

As part of this effort, TSMC is recruiting 300 new university graduates and young engineers with one to two years of experience who are already eligible to work in the United States. Considering a recent Semiconductor Industry Association report that found that 20 percent of semiconductor industry workers currently have no college experience, TSMC may need to look past educational attainment to the skills required for success in today's roles and the ability to grow into future roles (SIA, 2021).

TSMC may also take advantage of talent intelligence to source R&D engineers, process engineers, equipment engineers, and IT software engineers from other engineering disciplines. It might also consider tapping engineers who have the right expertise but may be new to the semiconductor manufacturing industry in general.

Semiconductor manufacturing labor shortages have led to numerous supply chain issues, with global companies delaying the production of new mobile devices, cars, and smart machines because there aren't enough chips to go around. TSMC's new plant is only as effective as the humans who operate it, and the organization will be well served to be both creative and proactive about sourcing with the help of AI-uncovered skills adjacencies.

Financial services

As we mentioned earlier, the financial services workforces of yesterday were designed for a world where people walked into bank branches to make a deposit or withdrawal. Now, consumers are much more likely to head to the cloud to make an instant payment via their mobile phones.

The movement of banking online has increased the importance of industry-wide digital transformation. Mobile banking especially has accelerated the need for user experience and UI design expertise, as well as application development skills. The rise of blockchain and the evolution of payments are creating a need for skills like blockchain architecture, wireframing, e-payment, and Hyperledger.

At the same time, the increased use of AI and Big Data means that financial services organizations need professionals with training in Python, TensorFlow, machine learning, deep learning, Hadoop, and natural language processing. Cloud computing and open banking APIs are sparking a need for Amazon Web Services, OpenStack, and integration skills. Cybersecurity's growing importance means that new network security, DevSecOps, and cyber risk management skills are required every day.

The industry is simply not prepared. According to Boston Consulting Group, in today's typical bank, up to 90 percent of employees are dedicated to day-to-day operations, with only the remaining 10 percent devoted to change and innovation (Erlebach et al, 2020). But while financial services organizations have made significant strides in meeting the digital demands of customers, the industry continues to face challenges when establishing digital-first talent strategies, with only 15 percent of the top in-demand skills currently deployed within their IT workforces.

Four main groups make up the structure of the financial services workforce. About 45 percent of employees work in the customer-facing division of a bank, which includes functions such as sales, customer service, and advisory services.

Fifteen percent of employees work in the IT department, holding jobs in software development, architecture, and security. About 30 percent support operations to the front office, which includes risk management, financial control, and strategic management. And finally, 10 percent of employees are involved in bank administration, which encompasses the HR, accounting, and auditing functions.

Eightfold evaluated the current financial services workforce across roles, skills, and future readiness. We learned that one-third of front office roles are declining in prevalence, while most IT roles are gaining in prevalence. We analyzed the most prevalent skills in the banking sector, identifying each as either a "rising skill," "stable skill," or "declining skill." The top skills across all four groups are either stable or declining, which signifies that most financial services organizations do not have a future-ready workforce.

Let's look at the role of the credit risk manager as an example. Very few of the rising skills in 2010 were still rising in 2020. Tableau, Python, predictive analytics, and agile methodologies were among the many credit risk management skills rising in 2020 but not in 2010. This means that financial services IT professionals who were extremely qualified in 2010 may not have the right skills to hold these jobs today.

We've talked about software engineering throughout the book, but many people don't associate this role with financial services. Yet in this sector, software engineering is where we see some of the greatest skills gaps. Among the 2010 rising skills were jQuery, Jira, Apache Maven, JSON, C#, and AJAX. On the other hand, the 2020 list of rising skills includes react.js, MongoDB, Amazon Web Services, and machine learning.

As in the telecommunications and semiconductor manufacturing industries, banking and financial services can assess existing skills, upskill, reskill and cross-skill, and transition key roles through talent intelligence.

We already know that upskilling, reskilling, and cross-skilling bridge the gaps between rising and declining skills. In business support roles, for instance, data entry and GAAP standards skills are declining, while social media management and digital market-ing skills are increasing. In front office roles, cash management and call center support skills are on the decline, while digital sales and investment banking skills are on the rise.

By building upon adjacent skills, employees can be upskilled, reskilled, and cross-skilled into areas of greater need in the financial services workforce. Take a bank's systems administrator, for instance. This is a role that's declining in prevalence, but there are several rising career tracks that a systems administrator could pursue such as business systems consultant, cloud engineer, network engineer, technology manager, or DevOps engineer.

Using talent intelligence, we can analyze how the current and future (rising) roles are related. It turns out there is a high degree of skills overlap between the system administrator role and the cloud engineer role, including SQL skills, VMware, and troubleshooting skills. There are also many adjacent skills easing the path for a systems administrator to transition into cloud engineering, such as Java, Python, and Amazon Web Services. To take advantage of these adjacencies and close gaps, financial services organizations must be willing to calibrate roles with future-ready skills. Banks, like most organizations, tend to fill a job with a job requisition and a job description. The requisitions usually reflect the way the job has been done in the past, and financial services companies tend to search for candidates within the industry. Instead, they must tap into the emerging skills for each role. From there, they can seek these skills in each new hire or upskill, reskill, or cross-skill existing employees with these skills.

Let's explore the changing role of a product manager. A financial services organization can identify candidates with rising skills, or skills that are adjacent to rising skills. Rising skills for product managers include user research, rapid prototyping, and data analysis. These skills may be found in a financial services sector candidate, but they could also be found in a candidate in another industry, such as the technology sector.

According to the FinTech Job Report *Technology is eating finance*, "Despite the name FinTech, the job roles in these companies are quite different from those in financial services, and much more similar to those in technology companies. Transferable skills to get into FinTech are more 'Tech' than 'Fin'" (FinTech Job Report, 2021).

Another example involves the migration of the traditional bank teller role to the universal banker or customer relationship manager role. There's a high degree of overlap between these two roles, with skills such as customer satisfaction and retail banking integral to each. Moving to a universal banker role requires the addition of cross-selling, consumer lending, financial analysis, and small business lending skills.

Meanwhile, to successfully transition to the role of customer relationship manager, many bank tellers would need to upskill in the areas of business development, strategic planning, portfolio management, relationship management, and financial analysis. However, the skills adjacencies make both moves a distinct possibility, and depending on the candidate's potential, a likely reality.

Many financial services organizations also need fewer underwriters. But the underwriters they do have are equipped with hard and soft skills that will be valuable to organizations going forward. Talent intelligence can be used to help companies see how underwriters can be redeployed into other company jobs by, for example, improving their data analytics skills.

As in the telecommunications and semiconductor manufacturing industries, hiring for potential opens a much larger talent pool for financial services organizations—especially those that emphasize remote work and don't have geographic restrictions. By using talent intelligence to analyze candidates' ability to learn the most in-demand skills, the potential pool of talent increases sharply for any given role.

By analyzing business trends in target industries such as telecommunications, semiconductor manufacturing, and financial services, we can extrapolate how to use skill acquisition and development to combat labor shortages now and in the near future. It's a strong start with implications for other industries as well.

APPLY THE AI

FutureStrong has partnered with a telecommunications company whose CHRO has asked your advice on closing its IT skills gap. Right now, the company does not have the technology talent in house to effectively build the 5G, and later 6G, capability. The partner company's job requisitions sit online for months while many existing technology staff worry that their jobs are becoming obsolete.

How might you recommend the partner company use talent intelligence and the principle of skill adjacency to broaden the pool of internal and external candidates who are up to the 5G task? Write your ideas here.

Chapter summary

- All **labor shortages** aren't created equal. While economists and policymakers debate whether the economy at large faces a shortage of qualified workers, data shows that it's really a **handful of sectors** having the most trouble finding employees—including manufacturing, utilities, and business and financial services.

- The **telecommunications** industry has a greater ability to build out some skill areas more than others. While the industry is poised to improve its capabilities for cloud and edge computing and Big Data, our analysis identified low workforce readiness in areas such as 5G and Open RAN.

- Telecommunications can develop its workforce of tomorrow by **calibrating roles** with the skills of the future. By envisioning what a specific role might look like in the next 5 to 10 years, a recruiter could include rising skills at the most forward-thinking companies in its job description and requisition.

- Creating new **semiconductor manufacturing** capacity would be challenging enough if the work were limited to building new plants. But semiconductor companies also face disruption of the work itself, as changes wrought by **automation** create higher demand for certain skills and roles while pushing others toward obsolescence.

- While **financial services** organizations have made significant strides in meeting the digital demands of customers, the industry continues to face challenges when establishing **digital-first talent strategies**, with only 15 percent of the top in-demand skills currently being employed within their IT workforces.

- All three target industries can use talent intelligence to better understand the **commonalities and interrelationships between various job roles and skill sets.** This technology offers new insights to hiring managers, who can then focus on candidates with the capacity to learn quickly and grow into a necessary role.

8

Taking talent intelligence
into the future

On an airplane the other day, Kamal wondered if there could be a better model for how service companies operate. He talked with Alexandra, who shared her vision of rapid talent assembly. Rapid talent assembly is a model in which organizations tap skilled individuals from a large pool of talent to come together as a project team, accomplish a specific business task, and then disband.

Throughout this book, we've covered how to match skills with jobs, and the next frontier is matching teams with jobs. We want to use talent intelligence to enable the right combination of people to perform a task based on our knowledge of the individuals—whether they are superstars or team players—and the work itself.

In the process of tapping people for certain roles, we also want to move entitlement mode to empowerment mode. What do we mean by this? Well, for one thing, why should a single hiring manager get to decide who gets a plum role and who doesn't? Talent intelligence gives us transparency around who can do what, democratizes opportunity, and helps take the fear and uncertainty out of trying something new.

Once we normalize moving around, we need to ask the question: what drives upskilling at scale? To answer this, we'll need to understand how long it takes for people at varying skill levels to complete a task, and how much classroom content versus job experience is needed to do a task proficiently. If we can determine these details, with the help of talent intelligence, we'll have the basis of a Point A to Point B formula for any given task, and gradually we will put together a comprehensive blueprint for transitioning anyone—from anywhere—into a role. These ideas may sound lofty, but they are actually well within our collective grasp, and the rest of this chapter describes some of the plans to get there.

We've spent the last seven chapters learning about how talent intelligence can help you attract and retain talent in a tight labor market—whether you are in a public- or private-sector organization. Remember the challenging perspectives shared by our characters in Chapter 1? We'd like to recap how new technology implementations can get our CEO, CHRO, employee, candidate, citizen, and veteran moving in the right direction.

We'll follow that by introducing you to the Global Workforce Intelligence Project, our global, multi-organization initiative, and will conclude with some ideas for taking the first steps in implementing talent intelligence—and gaining leadership buy-in for your new approach.

Solutions across the workforce

The CEO

Liva is at the helm of a large manufacturing supply company headquartered in the United States. After a recent acquisition, she lacks the data to understand the skills that currently exist in her organization, and she's unable to locate new hires with the skills to maintain her competitive position.

Liva can adopt a single source of talent intelligence that combines both internal and external talent data to understand her workforce's skills and potential, as well as the market shifts that impact her ability to hire. By deploying a platform that can learn from every talent decision at the company, Liva can calibrate roles and match candidates with greater and greater accuracy.

The CHRO

Dennis reports to the CEO of his 55,000-person food and beverage company based in the UK. In the new hybrid work environment, Dennis realizes that his learning portal is no longer enough to retain his top people. Dennis can implement a personalized career management platform that directs employees to career paths in which they can be successful and encourages them to stay with the company. In pursuing this course, Dennis can become known as the CHRO who aligned talent with the business and built a culture of employee growth and opportunity.

The employee

Maria works as an accountant for a large healthcare organization. She wants to remain valuable internally and thinks she might want to explore different functional domains but lacks an understanding of how to transition to a new area. A high performer, Maria thinks she might do better elsewhere. If her company were to adopt talent intelligence, her leaders would have more visibility into her capabilities and preferences. And Maria herself could use such technology to apply her skills to in-demand areas inside the company.

The candidate

Damen is a graphic designer who has been laid off and is burned out on the job market. He doesn't know if there's a skill he needs to strengthen or a better way to present his experience—and is also concerned about bias in the recruitment process. Damen can apply to organizations that use talent intelligence for talent acquisition. When Damen types in his skills or uploads his resume, the platform will learn from his responses and make suggestions for how he might proceed. If the same systems contain equal opportunity algorithms that solve for bias, so much the better.

The veteran

Peter has worked as an officer in the US Navy for over two decades. But as he attempts to write a resume, he doesn't understand all he has to offer the civilian world. By engaging with talent intelligence technology adopted in the public sector, Peter can translate his military leadership skills to civilian functions such as business development and project management. And once the system takes note of Peter's skills, it can recommend opportunities to try out a variety of careers inside either one or multiple organizations.

The citizen

Elizabeth has a job in warehouse logistics for a multi-purpose e-commerce company, but because she doesn't have a college degree, Elizabeth's company is reluctant to promote her. She's considering moving to a neighboring US state with more opportunities to grow her career. Elizabeth's company can adopt a smarter approach to succession planning by identifying potential leaders based on skills rather than specific experiences or education. If Ohio doesn't want to lose Elizabeth, it could launch a state-sponsored job board that hunts for skills within individual profiles and matches them with skills in job descriptions posted by local employers. With a greater number of opportunities open to Elizabeth, perhaps the need to relocate will no longer exist.

SPOTLIGHT ON THE WORLD ECONOMIC FORUM

Collaborative pilot study revealed the "science of potential" among workers who may be viable candidates for in-demand roles.

The World Economic Forum (WEF) recently worked with Unilever, Walmart, and Accenture on a Future Skills pilot study that uses AI to map workers' skills and match them to emerging job roles. The pilot found that people have an inherent bias that causes them to underestimate their skill sets. The pilot aimed to close skills gaps by providing a truer picture of just how talented workers are and how they could transition into emerging job roles.

According to the WEF in an article about the study that appeared on its website, *Weforum.org* (Whiting, 2021), if you were to write a list of your skills, you would probably come up with around 11. But if talent intelligence assessed your skills, that figure would more than triple to 34—and it would likely open up new career pathways you had never considered.

The Future Skills pilot set out to answer three key questions: 1) Is it possible to identify and unlock hidden skills? 2) Are there more innovative ways to prepare people for the future of work? And 3) Do viable pathways exist for people to move between organizations?

The research team identified roles in 11 representative cities in the United States, Europe, and Latin America, which were then broken down into a collection of clearly defined skills. Not only did people vastly underestimate their own skills, but in some cases, a person would only need to pick up a few additional skills to switch careers entirely.

The pilot also showed that it would only take six months for people to be reskilled for new roles in completely different functions. An IT manager at Walmart, for example, already had a 50 percent match on the skill sets required to be a product manager!

It's possible to retrain for other roles, but most workers couldn't identify these on their own. So upskilling isn't just about training, but about helping people to spot opportunities. "Based on people's own interest and learning preferences, you can help bridge the skills gap in a very customized way," said Mayuri Ghosh, who manages strategy and public–private partnerships for the WEF. "It's no longer just about your degree or your qualifications, it's a culture and mindset shift."

The Global Workforce Intelligence (GWI) Project

After learning how our personas fair, the next logical question is: how can we achieve these outcomes for organizations, governments, and individuals on a bigger stage?

Last year, we talked with our partners at the Bersin Group about how companies across industries can't necessarily be compared to each other, because people practices, cultures, organization models, and rewards are different by design. Using talent intelligence to provide a global data set of billions, we are working with the Bersin Group to study the talent profiles of the world's largest and most successful companies. Breaking it down further, we are identifying the job models, skills, and organization structures that are most important in specific industries.

The target organizations perform well in three areas: financial growth and profitability, human capital excellence, and innovation and market leadership. Our research is focused on the following five dimensions, as outlined in the Bersin Group's white paper about the initiative excerpted below (Josh Bersin Company, 2022). Hopefully, based on what you've read in *Deep Talent* so far, much of this is familiar.

Skill profiles

The first and most obvious challenge companies face is a lack of critical skills. Business and technology skills are constantly changing. Most taxonomies encompass more than 50,000 skills ranging from technical skills such as "Java programming" to broad skills like "design thinking" and "financial analysis." Our research with the Bersin Group uses talent intelligence to identify the inventory of required skills across each industry segment, focusing on the skills that are growing in volume and importance, those that are declining or becoming obsolete, and new skills that seem to be emerging from nowhere.

In the last chapter, we talked about the upskilling challenges for telecommunications companies caused by the emergence of 5G. As part of the GWI Project, we've decoded many of the 5G skills needed to succeed, and have mapped them against skills required for 4G, LTE, and other older telecommunications systems.

Were you interested in how we identified skills that were rising, declining, and emerging in the three industries we profiled in Chapter 7? Through the GWI, we are researching several more industries, which we will report on in the near future. However, you can get a head start by gathering a cross-functional group and dialoguing about the "status" of skills within your organization. See if you can use your collective brainpower to come to a consensus on skills that are in, out, and somewhere in between.

Career pathways

As companies struggle to recruit and develop people to meet new skill needs and job models, we see enormous capability gaps in all industries. In response, some companies are building what we call capability academies to develop hard-to-come-by skills. Capital One created its own cloud-engineering academy in the past five years, primarily to avoid having to recruit engineers from Google or Facebook. Bloomberg did something similar in data science and analytics, and many healthcare companies are now building academies and even colleges to teach nursing.

But once you build this infrastructure, how do you find the right people to reskill into the desired roles? Our second step in the GWI Project will build career pathways for these skills. A career pathway is not a traditional career path through which someone may move from "junior engineer" to "engineer" to "senior engineer" to "engineering manager." Instead, it's a series of developmental steps to progress from one career to another. For example, a financial audit manager might become a cybersecurity specialist and go on to manage a cybersecurity team.

A talent intelligence platform demonstrates that many skills are adjacent to higher-paying jobs. You may have studied mathematics and statistics as an undergraduate, drifted into learning about psychology in graduate school, and then landed a job as an industrial psychologist in HR. While that's a great job, there could be a much bigger career for you in data science.

When one of the Bersin Group's clients, a large financial services company, was searching for data science and machine learning specialists, it discovered that many of its marketing managers had degrees in mathematics, the sciences, and statistics. The company built career pathways for those managers and, over the next 18 months, offered them new careers in data science—nearly doubling their salaries.

As another example, many retailers are scrambling to hire or train technicians and pharmacists for their fast-growing pharmacy businesses. We're developing a series of career pathways modeled after large healthcare providers. In many cases, people require additional education, job experience, and a few years to succeed—but this type of program builds employee engagement, company reputation, and a strong culture of growth.

Job architecture and job titles

We're also studying the job architecture of changing industries. In most companies, job titles and job descriptions are artifacts of days gone by. Companies tend to copy or guess at a job title (and description), often letting line managers make it up as they see fit. In fact, our recent study on organization design showed that only one in five companies write future-focused job descriptions.

The result at most companies is a hodgepodge of job titles, with many people doing the same type of work with vastly different titles, levels, and pay. This approach not only is inefficient but also prevents the company from building strong disciplines and clear learning curves. And it can have a negative impact on pay equity. The GWI Project will help companies identify these anomalies and develop an architecture for the future.

Furthermore, as we look at job titles and structures in each industry, we see vast differences between high performers and their peers. Going back to our financial services example, some banks have large employee populations in branch operations, branch sales, and IT service delivery. Other banks have a much higher percentage of employees in functions such as product management, marketing, engineering, and analytics. One could guess that the former are older, retail-oriented banks rather than newer, digital banks.

Finally, we see new job titles emerging every day. Marketing, for example, has seen an explosion in jobs such as "growth marketing manager," "marketing experience manager," "social media marketer," and "digital marketing manager." These newer titles often start as experiments for some companies but become institutionalized as functions grow and flourish. The GWI Project will illustrate these changes so you can see around the corner and plan where to go next.

Organization structures

The fourth part of the GWI Project looks at organization design as a whole. While every company is different—whether organized by product, geography, industry, or function—innovators are always pioneering groundbreaking solutions. For example, Southwest Airlines was the first airline to designate aircraft as an organizational unit, empowering pilots and flight attendants to essentially run their own businesses and make critical decisions independently. This, in turn, forced other functional areas in the company to follow and make each plane the accountability center for safety, on-time departure, and other measures.

As our research on organization design has established, clearly identifying accountability is the most important thing you can do to drive business outcomes and innovation success. Recall Alexandra's idea of rapid talent assembly. Put another way, many companies are moving to agile models in which people work on project teams, switching areas of focus from one period to the next. Individuals report to both project leaders and career advisers (often called "guilds," in agile lexicon).

Organizational design is undoubtedly getting more complex. What if your company is organized by geography but your biggest competitor is organized by industry? Does that company see something in the market that you don't? Or are you identifying geographic needs the other company is missing? Remember the supply problem in semiconductor manufacturing. Is it enough for a company such as Intel to build more fabrication plants? Or does it also need to reskill and reorganize to succeed?

If you just look at skills gaps and hire people to fill them, your operating model won't scale. The largest furniture manufacturer in the United States, for example, typically hired strong men to lift wood and handle manufacturing at plants all over the world.

Today these plants are automated, so the company needs centralized operations staff, operators, and digital monitoring—coupled with supply chain experts to keep the plants running.

Operating models are critical for internal business functions such as finance, HR, and IT, yet they're often designed on the fly. The GWI Project will include a deep dive into HR operating models and will then turn our attention to IT and other functions. By identifying the patterns of field leaders, among other strategies, we can better advise organizations on building the right operating model.

HR practices

For the final dimension of the GWI Project, the combined Eightfold and Bersin Group team will rely on our decades of HR experience to look at the talent practices of leading companies—including performance management design, pay practices, internal mobility, and methods of building leaders, career structures, and culture for growth. We've already observed that technology and pharmaceutical companies often pay 50 percent to 100 percent more per role than other industries, making it difficult for a telecommunications company or manufacturer to hire from these sources. Companies need to redefine rewards strategies to fit new industry models. By the time this book is published, the GWI Project will include definitive guides that cover these practices in great detail. We will also provide industry models and industry assessments to show organizations where they fit into specified maturity models.

SPOTLIGHT ON BOSTON CONSULTING GROUP
Global consulting firm identified where worker surpluses and deficits are likely to occur—and the role technology will play—in three target countries.

Boston Consulting Group (BCG) recently collaborated with Faethm, a firm specializing in AI and analytics, to study talent surpluses and shortfalls in the United States, Germany, and Australia (Strack et al, 2021).

To develop potential 2030 workforce scenarios in these countries, BCG looked at three components of imbalance: workforce supply and demand, technology adoption, and GDP rate.

The research team found that in the US, talent shortfalls in key occupations, such as computers and mathematics, are set to soar to over six million by 2030. So even though the country's overall supply of labor is projected to rise, the US will face significant deficits in crucial fields. In fact, the sum of all job family groups with a shortfall is 17.6 million.

Technology and automation will drive some groups out of work in the US, particularly in office and administrative support, where the surplus of workers will rise to three million in 2030. But for every six jobs that are being automated or augmented by new technologies, one additional job will be needed in order to develop, implement, and run those new technologies.

Because certain human skills like empathy, creativity, and emotional intelligence cannot be replicated by technology, the supply of talent for occupations (healthcare, education, counseling, etc.) that require these skills is currently limited, causing the high shortfalls we see in these job families.

In terms of an overall talent deficit, Germany faces the dual challenge of a birth rate that has remained low, at an average of 1.6 children per woman, combined with aging baby boomers who will retire in the next decade. Specifically, Germany is projected to have a shortfall of talent in computer and mathematics skills by 2030. The next most severely affected job family groups are educational instruction and library and healthcare occupations. Germany's general shortfall of talent does not preclude workforce surpluses: production occupations, for example, are expected to rise.

For its part, Australia will experience difficulties in filling jobs in certain sectors, although the overall workforce supply looks less stretched than in other regions. Compared with the US and Germany, Australia is projected to experience a substantial growth in labor supply. In 2002, the Australian national government started offering cash subsidies to parents of newborns in an effort to lift the country's fertility rate. The increase resulted in a baby boom of people who will enter the job market over the next decade. In Australia, the greatest shortfall by far exists again in computer and mathematics skills. However, technology will exacerbate Australia's workforce surplus in certain sectors including production.

Where to go from here: general and immediate next steps

Now that our time together is coming to a close, we'd like to spend the rest of the chapter reviewing ways to create a future with talent intelligence. This starts with both long-term and short-term activities.

In the long term

ENGAGE IN WORKFORCE PLANNING

Before you implement talent intelligence, you should understand the current size and composition of your workforce, and where there are gaps between the skills possessed by your existing workers and the skills you require to be successful. Using analytics programs, keep up with internal and external trends in workplace supply and demand and develop a plan for closing these gaps that maps to your overall business objectives. Ensure that you have the resources and budget to complete your initiatives in a timely manner. Whether you are in the private or public sector, don't keep this process to yourself! Along the way, solicit and incorporate input from stakeholders across your organization.

EXECUTE UPSKILLING, RESKILLING, AND CROSS-SKILLING PROGRAMS

Even if the current job market could support it, it would be difficult to maintain the hiring pace needed to source emerging skills from the outside. The fabric of every employee's day must now be woven with opportunities to take in-person and virtual coursework, acquire certifications and badges, and train on the job via project-based assignments, apprenticeships, and tours of duty. By fortifying your workforce with transferable skills—such as leadership, critical thinking, persuasion, project management, and applied technology—that are relevant across a wide variety of industries and roles, you'll have the talent available when you need it.

SEND A TOP-DOWN MESSAGE ABOUT LEARNING AGILITY

Starting with your CEO, your senior leaders should formally and informally communicate why continuous learning is a crucial part of being gainfully employed today. Skills change so rapidly that a single training program is unlikely to have much impact and an academic degree will probably take too long. Leaders and workers should be prepared for ongoing effort in shorter bursts and provide lifelong learning platforms and accounts to help workers connect their experiences and skills.

BROADEN YOUR TALENT POOLS BY STOPPING THE BOX-CHECKING

As we've mentioned before, a job requisition that requires a candidate to meet 25 specific criteria is not likely to be effective in a labor market where many roles stay vacant for months. Because candidates who are self-taught in certain skills often make the best employees, think about shifting your focus to hiring for potential and what the person is capable of doing tomorrow versus what they can do today. Also, given the proliferation of remote and distributed work, consider whether you need people in your home office (or any office) and if you can expand your search internationally.

UNCOVER HIDDEN WORKERS

A 2021 Harvard Business School (HBS) report indicated that tens of thousands of "hidden workers" are eager to get a job or increase their hours but have been hindered by traditional hiring processes (Fuller et al, 2021). These hidden workers may include individuals with disabilities, those who are neurodivergent, and those who were previously incarcerated. HBS classified hidden workers as belonging to three categories: missing hours (working a part-time job but desiring a full-time one), missing from work (unemployed for a long time but seeking employment), and missing from the workforce (not working and not seeking employment, but willing and able to work under the right circumstances). By modernizing inflexibly configured recruiting systems and incorporating talent intelligence, we can solve for hidden workers' discouragement while filling our open positions.

PREPARE TO CATCH DISPLACED WORKERS IN OBSOLETE OCCUPATIONS

Given how quickly automation is taking hold in certain sectors, there will be workers who simply can't keep up with digital transformation and successfully reskill to another role or profession. These workers may either be underemployed or edged out of organizations completely, potentially leading to a societal crisis. We each must do our part to assist these individuals in moving on. To that end...

BUILD LOCAL TALENT MARKETPLACES

Both public- and private-sector organizations can build digital career platforms that encourage constituents to seek out jobs and educational opportunities outside their current purview. We've talked about the benefits of using talent intelligence to add value to such an offering, but no one person or group can do it alone. Gaining buy-in is a process in itself, and the one with which you should probably start.

In the short term

A talent intelligence platform is an investment. Like many investments, its costs are felt immediately, while its benefits lie in the future. Consequently, not everyone on a company's leadership team may be immediately comfortable with embracing this technology.

To demonstrate the value of investing in talent intelligence, it helps to identify the benefits of the technology in concrete ways. That way, organization leaders and teams see how the new tools will streamline work, improve outcomes, and accelerate progress toward business goals.

When asked to invest in any new technology, the natural question from organizational leadership is: "What's in this for us?" Thus, the natural first step is to clearly communicate the benefits of high-quality talent intelligence, which include:

- accelerates and scales hiring;

- reduces recruiting and media spend costs (job boards, etc.);

- improves the candidate experience;
- supports quality of hire and diversity, equity, and inclusion goals;
- increases NPS scores for candidates and employees;
- increases internal hires and employee retention;
- conserves resources by using fewer point solutions (tool rationalization).

Much of the excitement surrounding talent intelligence comes from its scale. By seeking patterns and making predictions based on an ever-growing collection of billions of data points, talent intelligence offers an unprecedented view of how workers learn, develop skills, and adapt to various job positions or changes throughout their careers. Here, examples and case studies can provide valuable context.

You must also know how to describe why this technology is different from what's already in the market. Talent intelligence is a step up from traditional keyword matching, which cannot adapt its approach based on either the candidate's information or patterns identified in past data. Keyword matching is severely limited in that it only surfaces those candidates who happen to use the same keywords.

Then there's the exponentially greater speed and accuracy provided by talent intelligence. A talent intelligence platform that taps into various sources of information can more quickly identify the skills and abilities that are relevant in the moment, as well as how a candidate's application fits within this overall view. Faster, more accurate results can in turn help hiring teams make the right offer to the right candidate before that candidate accepts work with a competing company.

Your role as the informed leader is to educate. Outline how the new platform will provide these benefits because the connection between the outcomes and new tools may not be immediately clear to everyone on the leadership team. Your colleagues need to understand how technology influences key goals, and they also need to understand how humans interface with the platform, use its information to drive decision making, and see their own careers affected by its insights.

For instance, one organization we know built its business case on mitigating promotion disputes. Since the talent intelligence engine in question would be a primary source of making promotion-related decisions, the tool's usage would decrease managers' tendency to favor certain employees.

Once your leadership team is on board, they can actively demonstrate backing of the project. For instance, you can designate executive sponsors to participate in pilot implementations that your CEO can in turn share in open forums. This type of activity will ensure that the extra investment is being noted, appreciated, and aligned with the company strategy.

Even in the short term, a robust change management strategy is prudent. After all, AI tools are still relatively new to the 2023 workplace, whereas many of the old methods have been used for more than a century. For a new implementation to work, your people need to actually use the tool, and this requires them to change their habits. This won't happen on its own, however. Your formalized change management strategy might include a town hall presentation discussing the rationale for the new technology, an intranet dedicated to commonly asked questions, bespoke user training, and written pieces highlighting success stories.

Practically speaking, the organizations that have experienced the most success with talent intelligence typically re-architected their talent function so HR component functions no longer operated in silos. So, if you are considering a move to this type of platform and you are especially decentralized, you might consider restructuring before you undertake an implementation.

Don't get us wrong—a talent intelligence platform can be the foundation on which a holistic talent strategy is built. But merely purchasing a tool is not a strategy. Don't fall prey to the belief that new technology—even if smart and impressive—will solve all your talent woes. Often, this leads to the "spaghetti tech stacks" we see in organizations today.

The path ahead will involve a bit of bravery, a willingness to identify the weak points in your talent function and to reconfigure your people, processes, and technology to execute on high-level organizational objectives.

We hope you're departing this chapter with an understanding of how talent intelligence can help a variety of stakeholders achieve their goals, and how you can implement it on behalf of your organization in both the short and long term. Once you start, you and your fellow leaders are bound to see how much is truly possible.

APPLY THE AI

At FutureStrong, the 45–65-year-old demographic makes up around 30 percent of the workforce. Some in this group plan to take full retirement in the next few years, but many others are hoping to keep working and build their skills accordingly. Unfortunately, the path to relevant upskilling and reskilling at FutureStrong remains murky, and loyal workers are concerned about being left behind.

As the CHRO, how might you leverage talent intelligence inside your organization to target this group specifically? Write your ideas here.

Chapter summary

- A reskilling project by the World Economic Forum and partners showed that it would only take **six months for people to be reskilled** for new roles in completely different functions. But while it's more than possible to retrain for other roles, most workers couldn't identify these on their own. So upskilling isn't just about training but about **helping people to spot opportunities.**

- The **Global Workplace Intelligence research** with the Bersin Group uses talent intelligence to identify the inventory of **required skills across various industries**, focusing on the skills that are growing in volume and importance, those that are declining or becoming obsolete, and new skills that seem to be emerging from nowhere.

- A BCG/Faethm research collaboration found **talent shortfalls in computer and mathematical occupations** in three countries: the US, Germany, and Australia. In all three nations, labor surpluses exist in other job families such as administrative support and production.

- Even if the current job market could support it, it would be difficult to maintain the hiring pace needed to source emerging skills from the outside. By fortifying your workforce with **transferable skills**—such as leadership, critical thinking, persuasion, project management, and applied technology—that are relevant across a wide variety of industries and roles, you'll have the talent available when you need it.

- Build your case for talent intelligence by uncovering **internal and external trends in workplace supply and demand** and developing a plan for closing these gaps that maps to your overall business objectives. Ensure that you have the resources and budget to complete your initiatives in a timely manner.

- A talent intelligence platform is an investment. To demonstrate its value, it helps to **identify the benefits** of the technology in concrete ways. That way organization leaders and teams see how the new tools will streamline work, improve outcomes, and accelerate progress toward business goals.

Conclusion

Around the world, experts and professionals are claiming that we are in an age of uncertainty.

We aren't *certain* they're right. Think about it. During the dot-com explosion and downturn a quarter century ago, the future felt uncertain. Same with the 2008 recession. And it goes on.

The bottom line is: the future is always uncertain. We can't predict it; we can only prepare for it. And if you do nothing else to prepare, we hope you can develop a sense for the skills and potential of every employee in your organization. Without that, your people will quit for new challenges where their skills will be put to good use. Without that, you won't understand what people are capable of doing and won't upskill, reskill, or cross-skill them appropriately. Without that, you will continue spending millions on temp employment agencies when the work could be done in-house. Without that, you will keep laying people off who could be redeployed into the roles you have open. And without that, you will fail to *attract* top talent drawn to a skills-oriented workplace.

We hope reading *Deep Talent* is just the beginning of your journey with talent intelligence. You now have the tools to make this technology's promises concrete for the leaders and teams that will use the platform and its insights. Remember that stakeholders who see the connection between the new tool and changed results are more likely to embrace the platform—and maximize its potential.

Ultimately, even if we are living in an age of uncertainty, this can be a good thing—especially for professionals whose careers now have positive uncertainty due to the numerous different career paths and opportunities opened to them thanks to talent intelligence. Each individual has good reason to be optimistic, because talent intelligence has the potential to facilitate a meaningful career for everyone in the world. If we're looking, this technology will show us the people who can guide us along our employment journeys, the work to take on next to feed our skills and passions, and the careers we've always wanted but haven't known how to find.

As you see greater and greater results with programs inside your organization, consider yourself fortunate to be living at a time when AI will make a positive impact on the future of work. Although business and market conditions are evolving at unprecedented speed, talent intelligence gives employers the ability to quickly build required skills in their workforces.

We can't tell you with certainty what the future will look like next year or in the next decade. All we can do is help you control what you can—and leverage the tools you have—today. We hope you'll refer back to this book as you progress through the next stage of your organizational and personal journeys, and we look forward to hearing about your experiences. Good luck! We can't wait to see how far you will go.

REFERENCES

Chapter 1

Benevity (2021) New employee data reveals the gap between ambition and action in how companies address racial justice and equity, *Benevity*, benevity.com/press-releases/racial-justice-equity-survey (archived at https:// perma.cc/NSG2-94NR)

Binvel, Y, Franzino, M, Guarino, A and Laouchez, J (2021) The $8.5 trillion talent shortage, *Korn Ferry*, www.kornferry.com/insights/this-week-in-leadership/talent-crunch-future-of-work (archived at https://perma.cc/ T7JK-R2Q3)

Chodyniecka, E, De Smet, A, Dowling, B and Mugavar-Baldocchi, M (2022) Money can't buy your employees' loyalty, *McKinsey*, 28 March, www.mckinsey.com/business-functions/people-and-organizational-performance/our-insights/the-organization-blog/money-cant-buy-your-employees-loyalty (archived at https://perma.cc/AHD8-2D5U)

Cook, I (2021) Who is driving the great resignation? *Harvard Business Review*, 15 September, hbr.org/2021/09/who-is-driving-the-great-resignation (archived at https://perma.cc/G5AP-8NSS)

De Smet, A, Dowling, B, Hancock, B and Mugavar-Baldocchi, M (2021) The Great Attrition: What to do about the labor shortage, McKinsey, 13 December. www.mckinsey.com/business-functions/people-and-organizational-performance/our-insights/the-organization-blog/ the-great-attrition-what-to-do-about-the-labor-shortage (archived at https://perma.cc/WV5V-LC5K)

Eaton, K, Mallon, D and Schwartz, J (2021) Human Capital Trends Report, *Deloitte*, www2.deloitte.com/us/en/insights/focus/human-capital-trends. html (archived at https://perma.cc/D2PE-EJXL)

Edelman (2021) Edelman Trust Barometer, www.edelman.com/sites/g/files/ aatuss191/files/2021-03/2021%20Edelman%20Trust%20Barometer. pdf (archived at https://perma.cc/GTC5-LAYV)

Feeney, E (2021) 2021 Workforce trends: Spotlight on compliance, Corporate Compliance Insights, 18 March, www.corporatecomplianceinsights.com/

2021-workforce-trends-spotlight-on-compliance/ (archived at https:// perma.cc/EN2D-B9BE)

Gartner (2019) Gartner says only 29% of functional leaders believe they have the right talent to meet current performance needs, *Gartner*, 19 September, www.gartner.com/en/newsroom/press-releases/2019-09-19-gartner-says-only-29--of-functional-leaders-believe-t (archived at https://perma.cc/2WJM-UZ5U)

Gartner (2021) Redesigning work for a hybrid future, *Gartner*, irwglobal. org/report-gartner-redesigning-work-for-a-hybrid-future/ (archived at https://perma.cc/WT5C-29PK)

Heiser, T and Keane, J (2021) 4 strategies for building a hybrid workplace that works, *Harvard Business Review*, 22 July, hbr.org/2021/07/4-strategies-for-building-a-hybrid-workplace-that-works (archived at https://perma.cc/6D7L-AZ3C)

Kaiser Family Foundation (2021) 2021 Employer Health Benefits Survey, *KFF*, www.kff.org/health-costs/report/2021-employer-health-benefits-survey/ (archived at https://perma.cc/YGL2-H2ER)

Liu, J (2021) 4.8 million working parents have 'preventable' burnout—here are 5 things that can ease the stress, *CNBC*, 7 December, www.cnbc. com/2021/12/07/4point8-million-working-parents-have-preventable-burnout5-ways-to-help.html (archived at https://perma.cc/QP5G-GDEV)

Meister, J (2021) The future of work is employee well-being, *Forbes*, 4 August, www.forbes.com/sites/jeannemeister/2021/08/04/the-future-of-work-is-worker-well-being (archived at https://perma.cc/3KXT-KPJ7)

Microsoft (2021) Work Trend Index Report, www.microsoft.com/en-us/ worklab/work-trend-index (archived at https://perma.cc/LVN3-NFM8)

Olivier, C (2021) Give me workplace flexibility or give my organization death, *Fast Company*, 9 December, www.fastcompany.com/90704468/ give-me-workplace-flexibility-or-give-my-organization-death (archived at https://perma.cc/JY4R-B6C8)

Pendell, R (2022) 7 Gallup workplace insights: What we learned in 2021, *Gallup*, 1 January, www.gallup.com/workplace/358346/gallup-workplace-insights-learned-2021.aspx (archived at https://perma.cc/6652-7HQW)

Pickard-Whitehead, G (2021) COVID and the gig economy – by the numbers, *Small Business Trends*, 16 November, smallbiztrends.com/

2021/10/covid-gig-economy-statistics.html (archived at https://perma.cc/2ZJD-56DC)

PwC (2021) Global Diversity and Inclusion Survey, www.pwc.com/gx/en/services/people-organisation/global-diversity-and-inclusion-survey.html (archived at https://perma.cc/RCL2-G2LS)

Chapter 2

Albinus, P (2021) How chevron drilled into its HR data to tap new talent, *HR Executive*, 13 October, hrexecutive.com/how-chevron-drilled-into-its-hr-data-to-tap-new-talent/ (archived at https://perma.cc/BN2L-EJCK)

Alderton, M (2019) How gig-economy growth could help close the labor gap in construction, *Redshift by Autodesk*, 17 September, redshift.autodesk.com/articles/gig-economy-growth (archived at https://perma.cc/9F9F-A9K4)

González, C (2020) The future of artificial intelligence domination, *ASME*, www.asme.org/getmedia/0950b928-dce1-45f3-a069-0c4725c4f25e/0903_the-future-of-artificial-intelligence-domination.pdf (archived at https://perma.cc/WS3A-98TH)

U.S. Bureau of Labor Statistics (2021) Job openings and labor turnover survey, *BLS*, www.bls.gov/bls/news-release/jolts.htm#2021 (archived at https://perma.cc/ZN2V-L563)

Yildirmaz, A, Goldar, M and Klein, S (2020) Illuminating the shadow workforce, *ADP*, www.adp.com/-/media/adp/resourcehub/pdf/adpri/illuminating-the-shadow-workforce-by-adp-research-institute.ashx (archived at https://perma.cc/G4XQ-LUC7)

Youn, S (2019) Women are less aggressive than men when applying for jobs, despite getting hired more frequently: LinkedIn, *ABC News*, 7 March, abcnews.go.com/Business/women-aggressive-men-applying-jobs-hired-frequently-linkedin/story?id=61531741 (archived at https://perma.cc/BH23-3WP4)

Chapter 3

Bersin, J (2021) Fixing your job architecture: A new business imperative, *Josh Bersin*, 10 December, joshbersin.com/2021/09/fixing-your-job-architecture-now-a-business-critical-process/ (archived at https://perma.cc/T9V5-WHTE)

Chapter 4

Amazon.com (2020) Upskilling 2025, www.aboutamazon.com/news/workplace/upskilling-2025 (archived at https://perma.cc/BVY4-Z99U)

Atkinson, J (2019) How PwC is investing billions in digitally reskilling the workforce, *LinkedIn*, 30 September, www.linkedin.com/pulse/why-pwc-investing-billions-digitally-reskilling-joe-atkinson/ (archived at https://perma.cc/KRZ9-X6KT)

BasuMallick, C (2021) How PwC's digital upskilling program is preparing its workers for the future, *Spiceworks*, 16 December, www.spiceworks.com/hr/learning-development/articles/how-pwcs-digital-upskilling-program-is-preparing-its-workers-for-the-future-8/ (archived at https://perma.cc/A6KQ-2BRG)

Bersin, J (2019) Build vs. buy: The days of hiring scarce technical skills are over, *Josh Bersin*, 24 October, joshbersin.com/2019/10/build-vs-buy-the-days-of-hiring-scarce-technical-skills-are-over/ (archived at https://perma.cc/T53Y-AWD8)

Burt, M and Gormley, B (2021) Flexibility is key for employers and job seekers in a post COVID world, *iPolitics*, 15 March, ipolitics.ca/news/flexibility-key-for-employers-and-job-seekers-in-a-post-covid-world (archived at https://perma.cc/BF3A-H5JR)

Gupta, S (2020) Here's looking at the challenges organisations face in making employees future-ready, *YourStory*, 5 May, yourstory.com/2020/03/challenges-organisations-employees-future-ready/amp (archived at https://perma.cc/H39V-URTQ)

Gurchiek, K (2020) Some industries boost training in new technology, equipment during pandemic, *SHRM*, 11 June, www.shrm.org/hr-today/news/hr-news/pages/shrm-some-industries-boost-training-in-new-technology-equipment-during-pandemic.aspx (archived at https://perma.cc/656Y-RNTH)

McKinsey (2021) Mind the skills gap, www.mckinsey.com/featured-insights/coronavirus-leading-through-the-crisis/charting-the-path-to-the-next-normal/mind-the-skills-gap (archived at https://perma.cc/MZ49-LV64)

Ravindran, V (2021) Reskilling and winning in the new normal, *All Things Talent*, 21 January, allthingstalent.org/reskilling-winning-in-new-normal/2021/01/21/ (archived at https://perma.cc/T9M8-N7XZ)

Sweet, J (2021) Fireside Chat Virtual Session, Nasscom Technology & Leadership Forum 2021

Vander Ark, T (2021) The rise of skills-based hiring and what it means for education, *Forbes*, 29 June, www.forbes.com/sites/tomvanderark/2021/06/29/the-rise-of-skills-based-hiring-and-what-it-means-for-education/?sh=5607b9534fa7 (archived at https://perma.cc/U6WU-4XR3)

Chapter 5

American Sociological Association (2009) Diversity linked to increased sales revenue and profits, more customers, *American Sociological Review/ScienceDaily*, 3 April, www.sciencedaily.com/releases/2009/03/090331091252.htm (archived at https://perma.cc/2LF3-3QMF)

Forbes Insights (2020) Fostering innovation through a diverse workforce, *Forbes*, images.forbes.com/forbesinsights/StudyPDFs/Innovation_Through_Diversity.pdf (archived at https://perma.cc/G899-KQS6)

Hunt, V, Yee, L, Prince, S and Dixon-Fyle, S (2018) Delivering through diversity, *McKinsey*, www.mckinsey.com/business-functions/people-and-organizational-performance/our-insights/delivering-through-diversity (archived at https://perma.cc/KS6E-2NZV)

Larson, E (2017) Research shows diversity + inclusion = better decision making at work, *CloverPop*, 25 September, www.cloverpop.com/blog/research-shows-diversity-inclusion-better-decision-making-at-work (archived at https://perma.cc/CHK9-3ZCU)

OneTen.org (2021) OneTen launches technology platform to create and enable one million career opportunities for black talent over the next 10 years, *PR Newswire*, 29 June, https://www.prnewswire.com/news-releases/oneten-launches-technology-platform-to-create-and-enable-one-million-career-opportunities-for-black-talent-over-the-next-10-years-301321856.html (archived at https://perma.cc/5T6V-6GNB)

Sergott, T (2021) Using AI to block unconscious bias, widen the talent pool and increase diversity, *Forbes*, 8 June, www.forbes.com/sites/forbestechcouncil/2021/06/08/using-ai-to-block-unconscious-bias-widen-the-talent-pool-and-increase-diversity/ (archived at https://perma.cc/KG2G-YRRH)

Chapter 6

Benett, J (2020) A guide to attracting talent in government, *Government Executive*, 4 March, www.govexec.com/management/2020/03/guide-attracting-talent-government/163517/ (archived at https://perma.cc/NE5P-RCRT)

Blazejak, M (2019) Why speed of hire is so important in a candidate-driven market, *HR Daily Advisor*, 23 May, hrdailyadvisor.blr.com/2019/05/23/why-speed-of-hire-is-so-important-in-a-candidate-driven-market/ (archived at https://perma.cc/9TB2-D33U)

Centre for Equity Studies (2021) India Exclusion Report, centreforequitystudies. org/wp-content/uploads/2021/01/India-Exclusion-Report-2019-20-e-copy.pdf (archived at https://perma.cc/469K-EVDZ)

Edinger, J (2021) Indiana's Hoosier talent network folds AI into the job search, *Government Technology*, 10 March, www.govtech.com/workforce/indianas-hoosier-talent-network-folds-ai-into-the-job-search.html (archived at https://perma.cc/Q9J9-4RAE)

Heckman, J (2021) Opportunity to reskill federal workforce for AI jobs "underutilized," panel warns Congress, *Federal News Network*, 12 March, federalnewsnetwork.com/cybersecurity/2021/03/opportunity-to-reskill-federal-workforce-for-ai-jobs-underutilized-panel-warns-congress/ (archived at https://perma.cc/SD8Y-TM5N)

Kwan, C (2021) Australia to build data tool for tracking local workforce, skills, labour market needs, *ZDNet*, 6 December, zdnet.com/article/australia-to-build-data-tool-to-track-local-workforce-skills-labour-market-needs/ (archived at https://perma.cc/HQ6Z-7PP8)

Long, E (2021) How to develop transparent career paths for entry-level workers, *Training Journal*, 11 May, www.trainingjournal.com/articles/features/how-develop-transparent-career-paths-entry-level-workers (archived at https://perma.cc/94QX-CCNN)

Mission Square Research Institute (2021) Survey Findings: State and Local Government Workforce 2021, *SLGE*, slge.org/resources/survey-findings-state-and-local-government-workforce-2021 (archived at https://perma.cc/5HT3-5KNP)

National Security Commission on Artificial Intelligence (2021) Final Report, *NSCAI*, March, www.nscai.gov/wp-content/uploads/2021/03/Full-Report-Digital-1.pdf (archived at https://perma.cc/NW2R-SRFU)

O'Brien, A (2021) IDC TechBrief: AI-enabled talent acquisition in federal government, *IDC*, March, www.idc.com/getdoc.jsp?containerId=US45993920 (archived at https://perma.cc/FSF3-ZPB4)

Partnership for Public Service and Boston Consulting Group (2020) A time for talent, *OurPublicService.org*, August, ourpublicservice.org/wp-content/uploads/2020/08/A-Time-for-Talent.pdf (archived at https://perma.cc/Y4X2-9NC9)

Ramsey, M (2020) Hiring challenges confront public sector employees, *SHRM*, 15 February, www.shrm.org/hr-today/news/all-things-work/pages/hiring-challenges-confront-public-sector-employers.aspx (archived at https://perma.cc/S4Q7-L3GF)

Rocks, J (2021) State governments and the coming talent shortage, *Deloitte*, www2.deloitte.com/us/en/pages/public-sector/articles/talent-shortage-strategies.html (archived at https://perma.cc/9VLY-98QM)

Smith, C (2021) Government is hiring, but faces tough competition for workers, *Governing*, 1 June, www.governing.com/now/government-is-hiring-but-faces-tough-competition-for-workers (archived at https://perma.cc/QLF6-9PYU)

Vergun, D (2021) App aims to match Reserve, guard talent with DOD needs, U.S. Department of Defense, 29 June, www.defense.gov/News/News-Stories/Article/Article/2675967/app-aims-to-match-reserve-guard-talent-with-dod-needs/ (archived at https://perma.cc/YL6E-ACK2)

Chapter 7

Duffy, R (2021) The US wants to get better at manufacturing chips. That's no easy task, *Emerging Tech Brew*, 7 May, www.emergingtechbrew. com/stories/2021/05/07/us-wants-get-better-manufacturing-chips-thats-no-easy-task (archived at https://perma.cc/78DN-D6Y3)

Erlebach, G, Pauly, M, De Jongh, L and Strauss, M (2020) The sun is setting on traditional banking, *Boston Consulting Group*, 24 November, www. bcg.com/publications/2020/bionic-banking-may-be-the-future-of-banking (archived at https://perma.cc/BR9L-CG95)

FinTech Job Report (2021) Technology is eating finance, *CFTE*, 17 December, blog.cfte.education/technology-is-eating-finance-fintech-jobs-are-like-tech/ (archived at https://perma.cc/UXD8-9PSC)

Fitch, A and Santiago, L (2020) Why fewer chips say "Made in the U.S.A.", *Wall Street Journal*, 3 November, www.wsj.com/articles/why-fewer-chips-say-made-in-the-u-s-a-11604411810 (archived at https://perma. cc/VUY6-XLML)

Gelsinger, P (2021) Putting our chips on the table, *The Hill*, 12 April, thehill.com/opinion/technology/547635-betting-our-chips-on-america/ (archived at https://perma.cc/6V42-ARTH)

Kharpal, A (2021) How Asia came to dominate chipmaking and what the U.S. wants to do about it, *CNBC*, 12 April, www.cnbc.com/2021/04/12/ us-semiconductor-policy-looks-to-cut-out-china-secure-supply-chain. html (archived at https://perma.cc/S7YR-7ZWP)

Semiconductor Industry Association (2021) Chipping in, *Semiconductors. org*, May, www.semiconductors.org/wp-content/uploads/2021/05/SIA-Impact_May2021-FINAL-May-19-2021_2.pdf (archived at https:// perma.cc/U52K-FCC7)

The White House (2021) Building resilient supply chains, revitalizing American manufacturing, and fostering broad-based growth, *Whitehouse. gov*, June, www.whitehouse.gov/wp-content/uploads/2021/06/100-day-supply-chain-review-report.pdf (archived at https://perma.cc/6V2A-C4BA)

Ting-Fang, C and Li, L (2020) Taiwan's TSMC begins hiring blitz for $12bn US plant, *Nikkei Asia*, 23 December, asia.nikkei.com/Business/ Technology/Taiwan-s-TSMC-begins-hiring-blitz-for-12bn-US-plant (archived at https://perma.cc/SU9N-DVE8)

Van Dam, A (2021) The seven industries most desperate for workers, *The Washington Post*, 15 June, www.washingtonpost.com/business/2021/06/15/ industries-with-worker-shortages/ (archived at https://perma.cc/R7H8-T9GP)

Chapter 8

Josh Bersin Company (2022) The Global Workforce Intelligence Project, *JoshBersin.com*, joshbersin.com/gwi/ (archived at https://perma.cc/DP7W-6FCJ)

Fuller, J, Raman, M, Sage-Gavin, E and Hines, K (2021) Hidden workers: Untapped talent, *Harvard Business School*, 3 September, www.hbs.edu/ managing-the-future-of-work/Documents/research/hiddenworkers09032021. pdf (archived at https://perma.cc/H4NQ-C5SB)

Strack, R, Carrasco, M and Kolo, P (2021) The future of jobs in the era of AI, *Boston Consulting Group*, 18 March, www.bcg.com/publications/ 2021/impact-of-new-technologies-on-jobs (archived at https://perma.cc/ M33M-K9UD)

Whiting, K (2021) This is how AI can unlock hidden talent in the workplace, *World Economic Forum*, 2 June, www.weforum.org/agenda/2021/06/ jobs-work-skills-future-automation-ai/ (archived at https://perma.cc/ F7WS-VY7A)

INDEX

Printed in the USA
CPSIA information can be obtained
at www.ICGtesting.com
JSHW071727230124
55934JS00025B/354

9 781398 609549